TORRANCE PUBLIC LIBRARY

P9-CLR-845

3 2111 00957 1263

CARGO
SHIP
CRUISING

WITHDRAWN

A guide to the joys of sailing the world in passenger-carrying cargo ships

Robert B. Kane

with

Voyaging Pr

To order copies of *Cargo Ship Cruising* you may use the order form on page 107.
Mail it with your check for $12.95 to:

Voyaging Press
4122 Verdant Lane
West Lafayette, Indiana 47906

The cover photograph of SS Santa Cruz traversing the Panama Canal is of an original oil painting by veteran cargo ship passenger Milian (Bill) Engh our shipmate on our voyage to Casablanca and Egypt.

Copyright © 1997 by Voyaging Press, West Lafayette, Indiana. All rights reserved. Unless permission is granted, this material shall not be copied, reproduced, or coded for reproduction by any electrical, mechanical, or chemical process, or combination thereof, now known or later developed (except by reviewers for the public press).

International Standard Book Number 0-910711-01-1

5 4 3 2 1

CONTENTS

To the memory of
Bill and Grechen Engh,
shipmates and beloved friends.

1

To Casablanca and Egypt

It was 7 a.m. Sunday, June 21 as we left the plane for a jetway at Houston International Airport. Late Friday afternoon we had a phone call from the Houston office of Lykes Brothers Steamship Company telling us our freighter, Gulf Bankcr, was scheduled for departure the evening of June 21. The airlines were facing a strike called for June 22 and we had decided to give ourselves the cushion of a few extra hours rather than take a later flight scheduled to arrive in Houston at noon. We were headed for a six week freighter voyage to the Mediterranean and the next place we could catch the ship if we were too late in Houston was on the other side of the Atlantic Ocean.

Cargo ships are unlike cruise ships, trains, buses, and planes in many ways. One of these ways is the tentativeness of their schedules. The cardinal rule is that cargo is king. Passengers, if any are carried, are simply along for the ride.

Embarkation dates, scheduled ports of call, and disembarkation dates all are subject to change and sometimes are partially unspecified even after the voyage begins. If such levels of uncertainty are uncomfortable for you but you are still interested in cargo ship cruising then you should consider sailing in container ships. They tend to adhere quite closely to routings and schedules but even they may deviate if cargo and circumstances dictate. To give you some idea of the shifting plans leading up to our arrival in Houston read through this list.

- Our original booking was to the west coast of South America from New Orleans.
- On May 22 this voyage was canceled.
- On May 26 we accepted alternative booking on Gulf Banker departing June 14.
- On June 8 departure was changed to June 21.
- On June 12 departure was changed to June 23 or 24.
- On June 18 departure was set for June 23.
- On June 19 at 2:30 p.m. June 23 was still correct.
- The same day at 4:45 p.m. departure was changed to June 21.

Here is what all this did to our travel plans from West Lafayette, Indiana to Houston. Remember, a strike affecting air travel in the United States was threatened to begin at midnight June 21-22.

- Plan one: Fly from Indianapolis to Houston arriving at noon, June 21.
- Plan two: Take the train from Champaign, Illinois to New Orleans proceeding to Houston by bus or air.
- Plan three: Take the train from Bloomington, Illinois to Houston.
- Plan four: (The one we used.) Fly from Indianapolis to Houston leaving at 2:30 a.m.

We waited at the airport until 9 a.m. before calling Ruth Scroggins, a Lykes Passenger Agent, She told us Gulf Banker was in, the dock number where she was berthed, and that we could board her right away. We loaded our luggage and our groggy selves into a taxi and within 45 minutes were in stateroom B1 unpacking and settling in for our voyage to the Mediterranean. During the longshoremen's lunch hour we walked about one and one-half miles along the wharves of the Port of Houston. The port ranges along the upper end of a canal which leads from Galveston Bay inland some 25 miles to Houston. Between Houston and the bay lies one of the world's largest petrochemical producing areas. The canal ends not too far from downtown Houston with a turning basin since most ships are too long to be turned in the canal itself. We saw freighters from the United States, the United Kingdom, Greece, Japan, Liberia, and Germany as we walked that Sunday midday. We learned that Houston's port moved more cargo than any other U.S. port during the latest three month period. Not bad for a city not on the coast!

Gulf Banker had loaded grain at New Orleans, enough grain so that the ship was already riding low in the water. The main deck was only three or four feet above the wharf. At Houston she was loading bagged chemicals and heavy earth-moving and mining machinery. Five passengers were booked according to the agent. We met Bill and Gretchen Engh who came aboard while we were out walking. They were happily playing cards in the passengers' lounge when we returned to the ship. The fifth passenger was due to arrive later in the afternoon but he did not show; we never did find out what happened to him and so there were four passengers in all. About 3 o'clock a tray of deviled eggs and other snacks was served in the lounge and we met our captain who greeted us and chatted for a few minutes. Loading was completed at 9 p.m. and we were underway at 2 a.m. on Monday. At least that's what we were told. By 9:30 both of us were sound asleep in our stateroom after a night without sleep in airports and airplanes.

Bill Engh stayed up for the cruise down the ship canal. He said he had never seen that much petroleum industrial plant in his life. He wasn't exaggerating; one-fourth of our country's petrochemical processing is done along that 25 mile corridor. By breakfast time in the morning we were clear of Galveston Bay, past the barrier islands, and sailing in the Gulf of Mexico. The Gulf is shallow along that coast and buoys marked the channel for another two hours.

Our fellow passengers, Gretchen and Milian (Bill) Engh, lived in Edinboro, Pennsylvania, a few miles south of Erie. That seemed coincidental since we spend part of each summer at Chautauqua, New York which is only a short distance from Edinboro. That coincidence was dwarfed, however, when the four of us discovered that we had all grown up in the same Chicago suburb! The Engh's were some twenty years older than Bobby and I so we hadn't known them as children but Bill's grandfather built his home only two blocks north of Bobby's parent's home. Gretchen grew up on Taylor Avenue in a house that was less than 300 yards from the apartment I lived in from age one to eight years. We determined that she gave tennis lessons at Stevenson Playground during the years I was playing in nearby sandboxes. Three of us graduated from William Beye Elementary School. Bill, the *auslander*, graduated from Whittier Elementary School. We all graduated from Oak Park-River Forest Township High School and, even though the Enghs finished high school well before we did, we had had some of the same teachers. It is mind boggling to contemplate the infinitesimal probability of such a coincidence.

Our first port of call was to be Casablanca, Morocco, some 4672 statute miles from Houston: an eleven day transatlantic passage. The second day out was our wedding anniversary, the second time we had spent that special date on a cargo ship. What a grand way to do it! We came up on a small craft in the Florida Strait. Our captain characterized it as, "Another honest drug smuggler out making a living." I wasn't sure whether he was kidding, but when we changed course a bit to pass more closely the small craft sped away. I'm reading Churchill's *The River War*; Bobby is into Gibran's *Jesus the Son of Man*. We both brought many books with us because freighter cruising days provide plenty of time to indulge our love of reading. Bobby does most of her reading in the sun; I split mine among stateroom, shaded deck, and the sun. Fast walking is another daily ritual for us at sea. On some ships it is possible to circumnavigate the main deck which could easily offer a quarter mile lap. On other ships, either because of their design or the placement of deck cargo, we are limited to a u-shaped partial circumnavigation. No matter what the route restrictions may be we walk between three and five miles each day at a fast pace—about four miles per hour. Occasionally I jog rather than walk, but not too often. The decks are steel plates, not wood. They are washed down with sea water by hose or by spray or both. In the morning before the sun does its work they tend to be wet with condensation. In short, they are often too slippery to be safe for jogging. In fact, we have sailed with captains who have stipulated no running on the decks at any time. Fast walking is worthy aerobic exercise and it does combat the effects of the dining room. In addition to walking and reading we spend part of each day writing and editing manuscript. So exercise, writing, and reading are our principal activities while at sea but we also spend a good bit of time talking, playing cards, watching movies, and star gazing on clear nights. Bill was an amateur painter. Almost every nice day he had his acrylics, brushes, and paint boards out on deck. He liked to paint the ships he and Gretchen have sailed in and had a complete collection of them hanging in a bank in their home town. He usually did a painting of the ship to present to the captain during each of his cruises.

We are often asked, "What do you do all day long on a cargo ship?" In a strict sense the answer is given in the last few sentences; of course the details will vary for others and even for us from day to day. In another sense what we do on a cargo ship cannot be defined or described or even alluded to by reciting the activities we undertake. A lot of what we do is more deeply understood by considering what we don't do. Is freighter voyaging, then, just our means of escape? In part, it is. But it's more than escape; for us it is recreative in the literal sense of the word. The phenomenon is illusive to describe for ourselves let alone for others. For example, most seamen think we must be crazy to seek out cargo ship voyages. I recall fondly a conversation we had with a young engineering officer one balmy tropical evening. He and I used to give each other mathematical problems to solve and so we often talked after meals or during his off-watch hours. We were sitting on the main deck where we had found him reading a paperback and he was telling us about his family in Texas. In the course of the conversation he said, somewhat incredulously, "...and you two pay money to be here?" We don't want to spend all our time on a ship away from our typical endeavors; we just want a few weeks on a freighter to be a part of our lives on a recurring basis.

Our route to Casablanca took us around the tip of Florida, north in the Gulf Stream, and then around the northern flank of Grand Bahama Island to the north of Bermuda continuing on a great circle route just south of the Azores and into Casablanca. Americans are often surprised when they realize that the African coast in the vicinity of Casablanca is significantly north of Miami. There were lots of ships to see off the Florida coast and in Bahamian waters but as we moved further into the open ocean the number of sightings diminished. And as our route began to deviate from routes between the southeastern seaboard of the United States and Gibraltar the ship sightings dwindled to very few indeed. The day after passing Bermuda we saw only one ship at about 7:30 in the evening.

One afternoon all four passengers spent about an hour touring the navigation bridge and chartroom being briefed by one of Gulf Banker's young third officers. The navigation officers included the captain, a first officer who held master's papers and thus was licensed to assume command of the vessel should that become necessary, a second officer who held first officer's papers, and two third officers. Not long after this voyage Lykes eliminated the second third officer in one of a long string of economy moves in the futile effort to stay competitive with foreign flag shipping. By the mid 1980's the U.S. merchant fleet had only one-fourth as many ships as it had in 1950. We were actually paying Soviet shipping to carry some of our free grain to Africa! Gulf Banker also carried two merchant marine cadets-in-training. All the officers were young except for the captain who appeared to be in his fifties. We were cruising at 18 knots and were using about 8.2 barrels of bunker fuel each hour in quiet seas, more when the seas were up. On a lengthy great circle route such as the Casablanca run the routing is segmented into a series of compass headings. The heading is changed once each day, typically at noon.

Ship's positions traditionally have been derived by using a sextant to shoot the noon sun or selected stars at night followed by a set of calculations based on published tables, spherical trigonometry, and accurate time-keeping. The mathematics of position fixing remains the same, but the technology has metamorphasized. Gulf Banker was equipped with a micro-processor linked to a receiver which "shoots" orbiting satellites within acceptable ranges and prints out the ship's position based on these data. Routinely, between ten and thirty positions per day are provided by this system. Gulf Banker still carries a sextant but it wouldn't surprise me if most of the navigation officers were pretty rusty on its use and on deriving the ship's position from the tables. As this account is being written the technology is even more advanced. Now the satellite data are constantly processed to provide continuous position fixes available on a video display on the bridge. These fixes are accurate to within 50 feet in most parts of the world! Just a few sentences above you read that navigation was done traditionally with sextant, mathematics, and an accurate timepiece. True, as far as it goes, but there is much more to the story. Determining latitude, the distance north or south of the equator, has been done by measuring the angle above the horizon of selected heavenly bodies for a very long time. Columbus "sailed the parallel" across the Atlantic in 1492. What may surprise you is that there was no reliable method of determining longitude, the distance east or west of some reference. Throughout the Age of Exploration, the great historical sea captains had no practical means of determining longitude on the world's oceans. Vasco de Gama, Magellan, Balboa, Drake and all the rest were essentially "lost at sea" despite the charts and compasses they carried. In truth, they got where they were going by hunch, luck, and the grace of God. The quest for a technology to provide a means of determining longitude has been characterized as one of the great scientific problems humankind faced. Finally, by the end of the eighteenth century, timepieces accurate enough and impervious enough to the hostile environment of an ocean ship began to be used by the navies and merchant fleets of Europe and the infant United States of America and the longitude problem was solved.

On our fifth day at sea we saw only one vessel: a yacht running without sail about four miles to the south of our route. As we passed, the yacht changed course heading south. It was mid-afternoon and they were headed back toward Bermuda not far over the horizon. Gulf Banker, heavy with her cargo, had virtually no pitch or roll on the gentle ocean swells. I was pretty sure the occupants of that yacht didn't perceive the ocean as being quite as gentle and unobtrusive as we did. Our stateroom was a long way from the engine room and the propeller shaft bearings so we had fewer mechanical sounds in our room aboard ship than we do in our home. To heighten the quietness of a big ship like this one all you have to do is walk the main deck to the extreme bow of the ship. The propeller and its shaft bearings are a ship's length away, the distance from the engine room is maximized, and what remains is the sound of the ship slicing through the water—little else. It is a quieting almost temple-like environment on a calm morning or evening. Late at night, with the ship darkened everywhere forward of the navigation bridge, the ship's bow is a beautiful place to be. However, when the wind is up and the seas are rough, the bow offers a very different environment. The pitch and roll of the ship, the smash of the hull into the waves, and the spray washing over the most forward deck areas all suggest that you leave this part of the ship to the elements until quieter weather conditions return. We expect to return to the United States empty and Gulf Banker, light on fuel as well, should ride like a cork on the water. Mid-level winds and seas could have us rocking and rolling our way home particularly when the wind is coming into an aft quarter.

On our seventh day at sea we saw two sailing yachts, one in the morning at long distance to the south and the other at dusk close in on the starboard side. One of the mates talked by radio to the second yacht as we overtook her. She was heading for the Azores from the east coast of the United States. The yacht's crew hadn't seen another vessel for six days and reported that they were one of five sailboats making the crossing. Later the same day we marked 2300 miles remaining to Casablanca. The sea was developing a few white caps compared to its glassy calm of the prior two days, but it was still an easy ride. Gulf Banker's roll was less than ten degrees in amplitude; very slight.

Another question we are always asked is, "What is the food like on a cargo ship?" We have sailed in freighters over the past 17 years and the most accurate general comment we can make is that the food has been very good; not outstanding, not gourmet, not grossly overdone as on the seven meal a day cruise ships; but very good. Passengers eat the same food as the officers and crew and they tend to eat well. Gulf Banker was a typical Lykes ship in this respect. There was one galley which served two dining salons, one for the officers and passengers and one for the crew. Breakfast was served at 7:30, lunch at 11:30 and dinner at 5:00 each day. Menus were provided each day and tended to cycle weekly. The menus offered choices for each course for each meal. Two stewards served the officer/passenger dining salon. The officers tended to sit in the same place each meal at tables for four arranged around the perimeter of the room. Passengers were assigned a table somewhat more in the room's center so, although officers and passengers shared the dining salon, they did not really eat together. The stewards took each person's order and the galley sent the dishes up on a dumb waiter. The food was good as stipulated earlier but it was served in an informal manner. Food was brought as it arrived from the galley: perhaps soup, salad, and main course all within a minute of each other. In contrast we have sailed in Yugoslavian ships where the passengers had their own dining salon and steward. On these ships there was no choice of foods offered and the steward served the meal course by course from serving trays onto each person's plates—a somewhat more elegant and certainly less chaotic service than was provided on a Lykes ship. The basic message is that the food is good to excellent. For those who like to snack beyond the three meal a day service there is always the self-service pantry and refrigerator open 24 hours a day. Breakfast, for example, on Gulf Banker could be a gigantic meal, a light eye-opener, or anything in between. One morning prior to reaching Casablanca Bobby and I each had apple juice, honey dew melon, a chicken liver omelet, and baking powder biscuits with jam. The noon entrees for the same day included Long Island duckling, beef tips, kidneys, and a ham salad sandwich. Clearly, our daily three to five mile hike was a necessary concomitant to the galley's efforts and, I must confess, to our occasional lack of restraint.

Two days were left to reach Casablanca as we passed the Azores. Santa Maria, the southernmost of these islands, was about ten miles off our portside so our view of its green mountain tops protruding above the surface of the Atlantic was limited to what could be seen through our binoculars. Our great circle route became more and more southerly as we approached the African continent. In the afternoon after leaving the Azores in our wake we had our second fire and boat drill. Everyone except the watch on the bridge and in the engine room reported to his lifeboat station wearing his life jacket. After roll call and an inspection of life jackets, belts, whistles, and flashlights we all convened on the starboard boat deck for a demonstration firing of parachute flares from hand-held launchers. The flare goes up about 300 yards if the launcher is held at a 45 degree or greater angle to the horizon and it burns in the air about 30 seconds. A fire and boat drill is held once each week throughout the voyage. In addition to muster and equipment inspection, each week some additional aspect of the fire and boat equipment and procedures arsenal was demonstrated or practiced. The day before we were due in Casablanca Bobby used the ship's washer and dryer so that we could hit the African coast with everything clean and ready to wear. We always use an elastic clothes line with attached clothes pins for any hand washing done in our bathroom. Most of our laundry is reserved for the washer and dryer which we used every week or ten days. We had a long talk with the second engineer after he came off his watch. He had been born in Honduras and lived near New Orleans. He had three children and talked to us about his wife and daughters for over an hour. In his spare time at sea he made macramé items; in fact, we have some of his work in our home which he made as a present for us during the voyage. He was hoping to make a deal with a merchant in Casablanca to buy caftans and be able to order additional ones for a boutique his wife and one of their daughters plan to open. As we turned in for the night we knew that Gulf Banker would reach Casablanca the next afternoon culminating a 12 day passage from Houston.

The name Casablanca was chosen by the Portuguese in the early sixteenth century after they captured, destroyed, and then rebuilt the city known to the Berber population as Finfa. Today it is the largest seaport on the Atlantic coast of Morocco. Revolts of the Berbers forced the Portuguese out during the seventeenth century and later, just before the onset of the American Revolution, Casablanca was again destroyed, this time by an earthquake. The French conquered the city early in the twentieth century after several European workmen were murdered while working on the development of its harbor. Perhaps Americans remember Casablanca best because it was here that President Roosevelt and Prime Minister Churchill met for their fourth wartime conference in January, 1943 not long after the North African campaign began the preceding November. Casablanca served as the principal supply port for the North African campaign until U.S. advances made feasible the use of Mediterranean ports thus reducing the overland transshipment of war material to the Allied forces engaging Germany's *Afrika Corps* in the desert. The two heads of state agreed upon General Eisenhower as Supreme Commander of the Allied assault on Europe and it was at Casablanca that they agreed to exact "unconditional surrender" from the axis powers. Of course movie buffs will never forget Bogart and Bacall and , "Play it again, Sam," the most famous line in the film entitled "Casablanca."

After arriving off Casablanca at midday we waited at anchor for four hours, then picked up a harbor pilot, met two tugs, and docked at 4:00. It had been necessary to wait for high tide to get in with our heavy load. Ten ships had been waiting in the anchorage; most of them were bulk carriers waiting to load phosphate. The others were container ships, a tanker, and the Soviet training schooner, *Tovarishch. Tovarishch's* twin, Eagle, was used by the United States for the same purpose: training cruises for naval midshipmen. Fortunately no other break-bulk ship was waiting ahead of us for dock space so Gulf Banker went right in. By the end of our first evening in port we had off-loaded eight huge earth-moving machines built by Caterpillar. The next day their monster wheels and power units as well as the chemicals we were carrying were off-loaded by mid afternoon. While the cargo was being worked we passengers spent our time ashore. After docking and an early dinner all four of us walked into downtown Casablanca. Our ship was berthed about one-half mile from the port gate which, in turn, was about three blocks from the central section of the city. The old Medina or Casbah or market section was on our right as we walked in and looked like an area to visit the next day. We changed some money at El Mansour, an elegant hotel, and Bill and Gretchen treated us to drinks in honor of Bobby's birthday. After we returned to the ship the captain invited us to his quarters for drinks so we all celebrated her natal day again! Our captain urged Bobby and me not to attempt a round trip to Rabat by train the next day. We have found that captains get nervous if passengers stray too far from the port if the ship is scheduled to leave the same day. Part of this concern is, I'm sure, motivated by the desire to avoid any hassle for them and the ship. In any event, we decided to forego the Rabat excursion even though the railroad station was convenient to the port and trains were scheduled in such a way that we could have made it back easily (assuming no major foul-up on the Moroccan railroad). The next morning we located the city tourist office, changed some money, and found out how to get to the cathedral and the beaches at Ain Diab. Bill and Gretchen opted for a taxi tour of Casablanca and drove off with Ben, an English-speaking guide. Bobby and I walked to the cathedral only to find that it was not open. Early in our walk I gave a coin to a small child who was begging along the sidewalk. I won't say that was a mistake because I don't think it was but it unleashed a very disturbing sequence of events. For the next two or three blocks we were literally besieged by children, mothers, and grandmothers walking with us imploring us to give to them as well. We gave them all our coins and a small bill or two; Bobby gave them some soap she was carrying in her purse. At that point we were out of things to give but convincing those poor people of that was painfully difficult. We know that begging can be a selected occupation and, I suppose, these people may have been professionals, but maybe they weren't. Perhaps they were as poor and downtrodden as they seemed. Should we have done more? Should we have ignored them from the start? These questions still arise when we relive the episode. I don't have any sage advice for you when you face similar circumstances. Whether or not these folks were truly in abject need or conning us mightily I know I wouldn't want to trade my life for theirs. ...But for the grace of God...

Late in the morning we ran into Gretchen and Bill still with Ben, their guide. We rode back to the Tourist Office with them and they then headed back to the ship. Their driver took us to the new cathedral and then up the coast road to Miami Beach Resort at Ain Diab. Although there was no ocean swimming due to the rocks and the power of the surf pounding onto the shore, the beach was quite nice. There was a large swimming pool, volleyball and basketball courts, showers, changing rooms, a snack bar, shaded shelters scattered across the sand, and a jetty out into the ocean. A lot of people were there, but not so many that we felt the least bit crowded. After two or three hours we taxied back as far as a large aquarium which we wanted to visit. Then we walked about three miles back to the ship stopping to shop for some gifts in the Casbah including one for Gretchen's birthday coming up in less than two weeks. Shortly after dinner Gulf Banker was underway. We watched the sun set as the skyline of Casablanca became less and less distinct. The Rock of Gibraltar at 6 a.m. was projected by one of the cadet officers.

During breakfast the haze was still too dense to see the Rock but there were lots of ships in sight since all traffic in and out of the Mediterranean Sea's western end must pass through this strait. By midday Gulf Banker had been spruced up following her call at Casablanca. The decks were hosed, the lumber from the deck cargo was stacked, scrap was tossed over the side, hoists were all nested in their cradles, wire ropes were in their sea-going positions, and hawsers for tying on to the dock were dried and stored. Gulf Banker was headed for the eastern Mediterranean, for Egypt to be more exact, but whether to Alexandria or Port Said was still unknown. Both ports are known for keeping ships waiting in their anchorages for extended periods of time. No doubt we would go to whichever port offered the shorter wait. In less than four full days we would be at one or the other. Ship's scuttlebutt said we would be a week at anchor followed by eight days unloading at dockside; a bit more time would tell. With less than two days to go we heard the decision: we were going to Port Said. Not docking at Alexandria was a disappointment because there is much to see and do there and we had information on how to travel between Alexandria and Cairo. On the other hand Port Said is the northern terminus of the Suez Canal which could provide much of interest to freighter buffs like us. The captain's estimates were four or five days at anchor (compared to two weeks at Alexandria) and one week at dockside. We began to think about leaving the ship and traveling to Cairo and then up the Nile to Luxor which is across the river from the Valley of the Kings. Of course unknown at that stage were: (1) How long at anchor, (2) Could we leave the ship while at anchor, (3) How long would it really take to unload a ship full of 50 kilogram sacks of flour, and (4) Who should we contact about arranging travel in Egypt? It was time to invoke the recipe for good mental health while cargo ship cruising: stay loose, don't expect to be able to plan everything in advance, and enjoy each turn of events as it emerges. The ship will do whatever seems best with regard to its cargo. Passengers, if they are to remain content, must go with that flow.

Gulf Banker anchored some seven miles off Port Said early in the evening. There were at least 80 ships at anchor with us. During the early morning many of them formed up in convoy for passage through the Suez Canal. Our hope was that our anchorage would be changed quickly to one close enough that we could be cleared for shore and obtain launch service to the quay. Just before breakfast it looked as though our hope would be fulfilled. We weighed anchor, started in, picked up a pilot, and finally tied down at 9:00. We had steamed just past the center of Port Said's water front and ended up along the east bank of the mouth of the Canal opposite the city. Our bow was held in place by dropping our anchor; our stern was tied to the shore. There was room, both to port and starboard, to bring in barges to off-load our cargo. And while doing it that way meant double handling all that flour several ships were being worked along the east bank in just such a manner. Regular scheduled launch service to the west bank and the city was announced and the schedule was posted near the lowered gangway. All four of us passengers took the 12:30 launch . A man who said he was the ship's agent (I never was sure that was an accurate claim) met us at the launch dock and took us to Misr Travel, a company with offices throughout Egypt, where we learned we must have a letter from Gulf Banker's captain to start the machinery going for permission to travel in Egypt beyond the Port Said area. The agent took Bobby and Gretchen to his "brother's" store as well as other shops in the vicinity while Bill and I made a special launch trip back to the ship for the necessary document (original and three copies, of course). Needless to say we tried to hurry. Not only did it seem important to negotiate the bureaucratic formalities with dispatch (an admittedly American reaction) but it also seemed important not to leave Bobby and Gretchen in the hands of the merchant "brother" any longer than necessary. We were clearly husbands with insufficient faith in spousal sales resistance. Armed with the requisite letter we all returned to Misr's office and planned our itinerary. We wanted to spend a day in Cairo and then take the new train to Luxor to visit the Valley of the Kings. Misr was pushing air travel from Cairo to Luxor and return but we held firm on using the railroad. I had read about the new train built by Wagonlits, the European builder and operator of top of the line railroad passenger and dining cars, which was in service between Cairo and Aswan. It sounded really nice and we wanted to see more than would be possible by air. Within an hour all was arranged. The four of us would be driven from Port Said to the hotel in Cairo arriving in time for dinner. The next day we were free to visit the museums and the pyramids leaving on the train for Luxor in the early evening. We would arrive in Luxor early the next morning, go to our hotel and then on to the Valley of the Kings. The evening of the following day we would take the train back to Cairo, be met at the railroad station, and be driven back to Port Said. Also included in the package were dinner and breakfast in Cairo and in Luxor.

And so we were off! The trip to Cairo was our first experience with Egyptian driving styles. The roads were mostly two lanes wide but we soon learned that two lane roads accommodate three car widths. When our driver wanted to pass or when we were passed by another vehicle none of the drivers involved worried about passing only when there was no on-coming traffic. Not at all! The passing car simply pulled out and passed with implicit faith in everyone else yielding enough space for three vehicles to meet and pass each other without touching. It was hair-raising for those of us who were not used to such a practice. It was particularly tingly when cars wished to pass in both directions at the same time. Two lanes may accommodate three cars abreast, but not four. Someone must yield or everyone loses. We also learned that brakes do not wear out as rapidly in Egypt as they do in America. There is a good reason for this; the horn is used instead of the brake in virtually every situation imaginable. We probably saved fuel too since we didn't seem to slow down and thus have to accelerate back up to cruising speed very often. We just got up to speed, used the horn, and passed cars at will. You've heard of white knuckle flights on airplanes, haven't you? All four of us could have attested to being experienced white knuckle passengers in our merry automobile between Port Said and Cairo. Our route took us near the Suez Canal to Ismaillya and then across the desert to Cairo. At Ismaillya a policeman flagged us down and after a brief conversation we invited his officer to ride with us to Cairo. I suppose he invited himself but we were happy to have him along and none of us seemed inclined to incur any ill will among the Egyptian constabulary. He spoke some English and so we talked all the way to the city. It became a bit embarrassing because once he learned that we were tourists (not that he hadn't figured that out already) nothing would do but that he would guide us here and there in Cairo. He wanted to take us to the pyramids that evening and to his father's home. On reflection, we probably should have done it but it sounded so much like the front end of a scam of some sort that we ended up insisting we were simply too tired to do anything but go straight to our hotel. If we had had more confidence in his motivation I imagine we would have had a good and possibly a unique time.

Our hotel was about two miles from Cairo's railroad station. There were no private baths and we started out with no air conditioning but that was an error and we were moved to rooms with window units. Dinner was reasonably good but when we had finished we were presented with a check for the meal. We had prepaid dinner and breakfast but we couldn't make any dent in the restaurant's certainty that we owed them so we paid the bill and then I took our complaint to the front desk. The misunderstanding was straightened out. We had ordered from the a la carte menu thinking we had free choice. The hotel deducted the fixed price dinner charge from the a la carte tab. Just another instance of communication breakdown across a language barrier. By the time all this was adjudicated it was 9:30. We went out on the street to find it teeming with people. The shops, cafes, and sidewalks were crowded as were the streets. Even the buses were packed full as they honked their way in the traffic stream. After a brief walk through the busy city life we decided to call our first day ashore in Egypt ended and went to bed.

After breakfast we took the courtesy bus to the main office of Misr Travel in downtown Cairo, picked up our train tickets, and walked to the Antiquities Museum. We hired a guide who walked us through the first floor exhibits talking at machine gun speed. In spite of his rapid fire delivery he was very knowledgeable and helpful. This morning we learned first hand of the persistence of the offers of assistance tourists must deal with in Egypt. We would have had to push through the swarm of taxi drivers and guides in front of the museum to have reached the doorway unattached. I can't be sure we decided having a guide was a good idea or whether we simply yielded to the insistent bombardment from all sides but before we entered we had a guide and we had a driver lined up to meet us in three hours to take us to the pyramids. After our whirlwind tour of the first floor exhibits we paid our guide and went through the King Tut materials on the second floor. The amount of gold was simply staggering! There was everything from full size chariots to jewelry. Just the sheer amount of gold metal was overwhelming let alone the priceless nature of the artifacts themselves. Unfortunately the whole experience was tarnished by the countless offers of guidance from person after person. Scarcely a minute would pass without being solicited. Even the museum guards got in the act. One beckoned us over to see a collection of coins and then insisted that we give him an Egyptian pound for his "service." I suppose I should have told him to get lost but I didn't.

We met our driver who first took us to our hotel to pick up luggage and passports and then to Giza for the pyramids and the sphinx. The driver pulled up in a small square very close to the open ground leading to the pyramids. There, of course, were the camels. "And wouldn't we like to ride the camels to the pyramids? No? Well then, surely we would want a picture with the camels. Just step over here... No, wait, you should sit on the camels for a proper picture." Can you see where this was leading? Gretchen was pretty tired and had already determined that she would see the sights from the verandah of a nearby hotel. Bill took her there. Bobby and I, poor fish that we were, sat on the camels who immediately stood up and started out of the square toward the pyramids. Bobby was really angry with the camel driver who by now was also mounted and riding with us. She couldn't get her camel stopped and jumping off the back of a moving camel was at least one step beyond the level of her frustration. It was at least five steps beyond mine. So off we went, the camel driver trying to change the topic from his deceitfulness to his adventures with Hollywood film companies on location at the pyramids and Bobby not cooperating at all. At one point the driver said, "Lady, you are giving me indigestion!" We didn't ask him how he could have indigestion in the afternoon during Ramadan since all good Muslims wouldn't have eaten after sunrise. About this time (we were about half way to the pyramids) Bill came trotting after us on a sorry looking horse! It must have been tethered nearby but I hadn't seen it. He had found a place for Gretchen to sit and was worried about what might be happening. Picture this: an aging American tourist who was no horseman bouncing across the sand on the back of a scruffy looking horse in pursuit of two other Americans clumping along atop camels while one of them, visibly angry, was being accused of inducing indigestion in the enterprising Egyptian camel driver. To anyone seeing all this and hearing all this it would have been hilarious. As I think of it now it was truly comic. We paid about one-fourth of the asking price for our camel tour and were glad to bid the pyramids and sphinx adieu. We really didn't see them the way we wanted to see them. Blame it on our foolish mounting of the camels and the Egyptian diligence in extracting all possible pecuniary good from the naive tourist.

We next visited a papyrus "factory" where we bought some souvenir prints on papyrus which we still enjoy and then it was back to the railroad station at 5:00. We were to meet a Mizr agent at 6:00 and our train was to leave at 7:00. There was a large waiting room containing scores of people but no benches. We finally garnered a table in the cafe about 5:30. We met our agent on time but the train didn't pull up to the platform until 7:30. By then all of us were very tired, very hot, and very thirsty. The only water available on the platform was running from an open pipe about a foot above the platform. Many people used that water while we watched; we decided to remain thirsty. Mercifully, the new train was everything we hoped it would be. It was sparkling clean, air conditioned, and beautiful. We were shown to our compartments and served bottled water icy cold. We left at 7:40. Dinner was served in our compartments soon thereafter and by 9:30 we were in our berths. Bobby and I were up at 4:30 the next morning. It was already light and workers were in the fields bordering the Nile as we sped past. Breakfast was excellent, again served in our compartments, and we pulled into Luxor only about 15 minutes behind schedule.

The town of Luxor is situated on the east bank of the Nile occupying the site of Thebes, an important city of ancient Egypt. Luxor is directly across the river from the famous Valley of the Kings, the site of many tombs and temples erected in ancient times. Perhaps the best known of these archaeological finds was the discovery of the tomb of Tut-ankh-Amen with its unbelievable mass of priceless golden artifacts by Lord Carnarvon and Howard Carter in 1922. We rode in a horse drawn carriage to our hotel, the Savoy, right on the Nile. Our rooms (air conditioned with baths) were ready and by 8:30 we had arranged for a guide to lead us through the Valley of the Kings across the river. We boarded a ferry, then a taxi, and then toured the tombs of King Tut, Rameses VI, and Seti I. Those were the ones we wanted to be sure to see but we had time to view several other tombs and temples on the west bank. The most impressive was Deim al-Bahri, the mortuary temple of Queen Hatshepsut. At noon we returned to the ferry landing by way of the Colossi of Memnon, twin statues representing Amenhotep III. The pressure to buy from peddlers at the entrance to every tomb and temple was wearying; I don't think I've ever experienced more persistence. We were there in the summer, not the high tourist season, so perhaps there were few enough visitors to make the selling pressure more intense. By midday we were ready to get out of the sun and into a more comfortable location so back we went to the hotel for a rest through the hottest part of the day. The air conditioning went off twice and our toilet wouldn't flush without dumping wastebaskets full of water through it—ah well, Egypt! Bobby and I went swimming at the Old Winter Palace Hotel pool, available to guests of the Savoy. Boy, did that feel good in

Luxor in July with the air temperature at 105 degrees Fahrenheit! The afternoon was marred by the near drowning of a man, a Frenchman we believe. He was dragged out of the pool and mouth-to-mouth resuscitation brought him around. No one on the hotel staff was involved! In fact, guests had to go to the lobby to seek help. It took 45 minutes for any medical assistance to arrive.

After a quite nice dinner in the hotel dining room we walked along the boulevard to the Etap Luxor Hotel a bit north of the Savoy and then back to bed; it was really too hot to make an evening stroll comfortable. The next morning we walked to Luxor Temple, only about two blocks from the Savoy, and spent an hour walking through its ruins. It covers several acres and walking among the pillars and statuary was really a great experience except for the barrage of would-be guides, peddlers and beggars. In the afternoon we checked out of the Savoy, stored our suitcases and went swimming again prior to catching the Cairo new train for the overnight trip north. The train was simply superb again and upon arriving in Cairo our driver was waiting for us. We made it back to Gulf Banker in time for lunch. She had moved that morning from the close-in anchorage on the east bank to a dock within the port along the west bank.

Now the unloading of 12,016 50 kilogram sacks of flour was underway in earnest. About 20 to 25 sacks would be hauled out of a hold roped together and deposited on a wooden platform some four feet above the dock. Of course the 20 to 25 bags had to be stacked and roped together in the hold to begin the process. From the platform a longshoreman would carry a sack on his back up a plank to a flatbed truck or trailer on which the sacks were stacked 15 high, about eight feet. It was back-breaking work in the hot summer sun. During normal operations each laborer would pick up a 50 kilogram sack (about 110 pounds) every 20 seconds! And this was Ramadan; for the faithful this meant no food, no water, and no smoking from sunrise to sunset. Ramadan or not, the laborers ate fruit and drank water. They couldn't have managed otherwise. The longshoremen's day began at 9 a.m. and continued with brief breaks until 5 p.m. They resumed work at 9 p.m. and stopped at midnight. Flour had been off-loaded into barges while we were away from the ship and for the first two days at the dock flour was unloaded onto trucks and trailers as described above and also into barges tied to Gulf Banker's outboard side. The last of the flour was unloaded 14 days after our arrival at Port Said's anchorage. During our days tied to the dock we walked into town several times shopping, seeing residential and commercial neighborhoods, and going to the beach. Port Said was a dirty city. Sidewalks were broken or missing altogether. Garbage and trash were everywhere and the streets looked like they never were swept.

Egyptians were always friendly and helpful to us but we had the feeling that everyone was trying to squeeze as much out of us as possible, and not only the peddlers, "guides" and beggars. Just one example: the ship's agent changed dollars to pounds for us. We discovered later that he was taking one pound for himself out of each $20 changed. Clearly that wasn't illegal since he was actually charging more than the official rate of exchange, not less. But we hadn't expected that sort of thing from a ship's agent. I told the captain later in the voyage and he just laughed. "That's Egypt!" he said. Another more serious impression we had was the abject poverty in which many Egyptians existed. There were entire families living on and around the docks. We watched women sweeping up spilled flour and grain off the docks to carry to their cooking pots. One day Bobby and I were approaching the ship after a walk in the city and we saw an old woman we had seen salvaging flour the day before. Bobby went up to her and gave her a small bar of soap. We had seen the crew throwing soap to people on the docks earlier and knew that it was valued. Before Bobby could turn away and proceed to the gangway at least four other women converged on her and in less than a minute five more were around her asking for soap or anything. She had only three small bars of soap, no food, and no Egyptian money. I had a few coins so I ran back to her, gave the women what I had and extracted Bobby from their midst. No one tried to hurt her; no one was angry. But the suddenness of the onslaught, the fervor of their pleas for whatever she might give them was shocking in itself to us. These people were desperately poor. The contrasts between their lives and ours, being lived out for a few days within 100 yards of each other, could not have been dramatized more sharply.

The 12,016th bag of flour was unloaded on a Sunday afternoon and we were scheduled to leave Port Said at 8 o'clock Monday morning. The chalkboard listed 7:00 as the latest time all were to be on board and the next port of call was listed as Haifa. What a surprise! The last we had heard we were going back to the United States with empty holds. Later that evening I asked the captain what we were loading at Haifa. He laughed and told me we weren't going to Haifa. That notice was posted to discourage potential stowaways! This led to a discourse on what a major problem a stowaway was to the ship and what a major expense he was to the shipping company. If a stowaway is discovered too late to put him ashore in his own country, the ship is involved in a lot of bureaucratic machinations and is responsible for all expenses involved in admitting the stowaway to the country of the next port of call, the expense of returning the stowaway to his own country, and usually a substantial fine. No wonder the phony message was on the board. The question I thought about was whether the savvy potential stowaway would believe that an empty United States ship was really going to Haifa. At any rate 8 o'clock came and went; no pilot. Ten o'clock came, 11 o'clock, noon... The captain was fit to be tied. At 12:45 the pilot arrived and was harangued by our captain in no uncertain terms. And so we bid farewell to Egypt. Gulf Banker was under way by 1:00 and 45 minutes later we were on the Mediterranean. Unless we received a radio message sending us for cargo in North Africa or Southern Europe we were headed home.

Our second day out the wind was up to force five or six and our empty ship was rocking and rolling along. The winds from the west were causing Gulf Banker to slam down hard into the on-coming waves and we reduced our speed to minimize the pounding. After a day or so the winds moderated and by the time we were in the western half of the Mediterranean the weather was calm, sunny, and warm—really delightful for cruising. The last day before reaching the Strait of Gibraltar the sea was almost like a millpond and the haze, common in those waters in the summer, produced varied visibility ranging from 400 yards to several miles as we glided along. After passing through the Strait of Gibraltar between midnight and 3 a.m. we were on the great circle route to the Bahamas but we had not yet been advised which U.S. port was to be our destination. The second night in the Atlantic there was enough roll to send everything not tied down flying around the stateroom. By morning the wind and seas had moderated quite a bit but Gulf Banker was still pitching and rolling markedly. During the crossing my birthday came up and I was surprised and really pleased when Bobby gave me a painting of Gulf Banker rendered by Bill Engh. It was a surprise because I thought Bill had no more boards on which to paint and I had really wanted one of his works. The seas continued to moderate and we had several beautiful days in a row as we followed the shortest route between Gibraltar and Florida. The word was that our port of disembarkation would be Houston but, not surprisingly for a cargo ship, that word was changed two days later. We were going to New Orleans, not Houston. Gulf Banker's next voyage was to be to South and East Africa and her cargo was to be loaded at the Crescent City on the Mississippi River. Bill and Gretchen prepared a note, sealed it in a glass bottle, and threw it overboard. Bill told me they had done this on each of the twelve cargo ship cruises he and Gretchen had made. They hadn't heard from anyone who may have picked up one of their bottles but they kept the tradition going. As we came closer to North America Bobby and I spent an hour or so each night

Gulf Banker, painted by Bill Engh, freighter buff and friend.

on the bridge roof under the stars. The night sky at sea is truly special, spectacular, to be savored. Were we trying to store up such memories in recognition of our forthcoming return to our "real" world? I don't know. One such experience is as memorable as twenty so I suppose we just did not want to waste any of those precious opportunities. Perhaps it is already evident to you: we have a love affair going with cargo ship cruising.

When we docked at New Orleans it was early morning. By 9:00 we were cleared to go ashore for the last time. Bill and Gretchen headed for the airport. Bobby and I were spending the day in New Orleans and leaving on Amtrak's City of New Orleans late in the afternoon. We wished the Engh's a safe trip; what wonderful shipmates they had been! Later they made the pages of *New Yorker* magazine and still later the final chapter of a book based on the magazine articles. These articles chronicled a freighter voyage from the perspective of a merchant marine officer and his friend, the author. Basically the writing was about the diminishing U.S. Merchant Marine so there wasn't much about sailing in cargo ships from the passenger perspective. But the author fell under the spell of Gretchen and Bill just as we had. Bill was still doing his paintings of ships while combating the cancer which intruded on his life. We were to see them once or twice a year in Edinboro or Chautauqua or West Lafayette until illness and longevity took them both from us within a few weeks of each other. Farewell Gretchen and Bill. You made freighter voyaging sweeter for us by your friendship and your spirit and our time together on Gulf Banker.

2

'Round the World with Containers

S unlight sparkled on the harbor waters as we drove over the Queensway Bridge joining downtown Long Beach, California to its port area. "There she is!" I exclaimed. Dark blue hull, white deckhouse, containers stacked in even ranks across the hatch covers, with ASIAN SENATOR in white block letters on the side of the hull near the bow. We had a map to guide us to the container terminal but I had looked up from it and away from the road signs overhead long enough to spot the ship which was to be our home for the next twelve weeks. We quickly found the container terminal gate, parked the car and transferred all the luggage and ourselves to a port van which would take us to the ship. The van driver hailed the ship's bosun, helped us unload the luggage into a large basket which the bosun had lowered to the dock, and while our luggage was hoisted aboard we walked up the gangway and stepped onto the main deck. We met the captain who took us to stateroom A which was to be ours as we circled the earth as supercargo with the containers which justified the existence of Asian Senator. The next visit we were to make to Long Beach would be after calling on 16 other ports along our route around the world. After putting all the luggage in our stateroom and looking around the deckhouse a bit we left the ship to do a little last minute shopping before returning to the port. Our brother-in-law dropped us at the gate saying he would see us in three months and Bobby and I approached Asian Senator to begin our first cargo ship cruise in almost six years and, more importantly, our first-ever cruise on a container ship. Asian Senator handled only containers; her capacity was 2000 20 foot container units distributed along her 596 foot length. This standardized packaging of cargo made loading and unloading far more efficient than was possible on general cargo ships. As the chief mate pointed out to us during the voyage, the only things a shipping company has to offer its customers are reliability and speed. Container ships in intercontinental service adhere as closely as possible to a schedule published well in advance of sailing which depends upon efficient docking and cargo handling in each port. This results in typical port times of six to 24 hours for container ships rather than the two to four days (or longer) for general cargo ships. Of course we knew all this before requesting space for this cruise. We knew we were embarking on a long voyage with lots of sea time. We didn't know how life would be with such short port times. Would we develop a modern day version of cabin fever? We were looking forward to finding out. We had loved sailing in general cargo ships; what would sailing with containers be like?

Our stateroom was large: about 16 feet by 16 feet. There were twin beds which could be reconfigured into a king-size bed. There were twin closets, two windows, one forward and one on the starboard side. There was a sofa, an easy chair, desk and chair, refrigerator stocked with fruit, soft drinks, and mineral water, a radio/tape deck, carpet on the deck, and, of course, a bathroom. We unpacked and filled our closets, drawers, and cabinets. What a good feeling it was to know that we didn't need to look at suitcases again for twelve weeks. The unloading and loading of containers, the loading of bunker fuel, and the provisioning of the ship continued throughout the afternoon and evening and ended in the middle of the night.

At 5:30 in the morning we sailed out of Long Beach's harbor and headed up the California coast for Oakland passing under the Golden Gate Bridge at 5:10 the next morning. We were on the bridge at 5:00 and we stayed there as Asian Senator negotiated San Francisco Bay and moved up the estuary which divides the mainland at Oakland from Alameda Island to berth number 69 at the container port. This was the first freighter in which we have sailed that granted passengers unlimited access to the navigation bridge. What a boon this was! All the communications and commands exchanged among pilot, ship's officers, helmsmen, tugboats, shore and ship's crew for maneuvering the ship in channels, harbors, ports, and in docking were available as a matter of personal experience; not just the results, but the process itself was shared with those passengers who elected to be on the bridge. Moreover, while at sea the watch officers were always glad to have passengers spend time on the bridge. We learned much more through having this unlimited access than we might have through the more common guided tour of the navigation equipment. The navigational reference books and journals as well as the charts were also available to us. This was a really nice feature of cruising on Asian Senator and we were careful not to abuse the privilege. Asian Senator, of German registry, carried a complement of 22: eight officers, six Germans and two Filipinos; and 14 crew, three Germans and eleven Filipinos. In addition there were five passengers: Carol and Bob, a retired couple who were former school teachers; Vivian, a widow; and Bobby and I.

Right after breakfast Bobby and I together with Carol and Bob made our way to the port gate and while they elected to look around Oakland we decided to take the Bay Area Rapid

Transit train (BART) to San Francisco. We walked through Chinatown and along the Embarcadero. We ate a light lunch and, after returning to Oakland, bought mineral water for Vivian, detergent, candy, and root beer for us and walked back to our ship. By 3:30 p.m. all loading was completed and at 5:15 the pilot and tugs were at hand and we left berth 69, moved down the estuary, across the bay, and under the Golden Gate Bridge. I stayed on the navigation bridge until we dropped our pilot at 8 o'clock. With the sights of San Francisco receding behind us we set our course of 278°. Next stop, Yokohama. The chief mate told me that we were not taking the shortest route along the great circle from San Francisco to Tokyo Bay. The ship used the consultative recommendations of Oceanroutes, a weather and course advisory service. Their suggestion for this crossing was to stay further south than the great circle course would have taken us in order to minimize the heavy seas and head winds predicted for the North Pacific. About halfway across the ocean we were to pick up a great circle course from that point into Japan. For the first few days we were to steer 278°, only eight degrees north of due west.

Ready to unload containers.

And thus we began the eleven day passage to the port of Yokohama nestled in Tokyo Bay. How do you spend eleven days at sea on a cargo ship? A specific answer to that question, a question we are frequently asked, depends on the season, the region, and the sun. Put another way, weather governs the range of choices. For that reason we try to select cruises which have a reasonable chance of offering mild to warmer weather, at least for a sizable portion of the route. Crossing the North Pacific Ocean in early April was that portion of this cruise least likely to yield delightful weather. So let's consider a generic answer to the question, "What do you do with yourself for eleven days at sea?" rather than list out a litany of day one through day eleven. We always make aerobic exercise a part of every day. Bobby does about 30 minutes of calisthenics before breakfast; I don't! We both walk between four and five miles at a brisk pace every day. Five miles on a ship? Yes; we spend no less than one hour walking the deck which offers the longest path available on the ship. On Asian Senator the main deck (named "upper deck" for no good reason we could tell) provided a perimeter of the ship route of a bit more than a quarter mile. Sometimes it was not possible to walk the entire perimeter because of painting or other work being done but, with few exceptions, at least one half the full perimeter was available every day. In addition to exercising, we write and edit manuscript for books like this one and we read—a lot! Bobby knits, we play cards (no quarter asked or given), and we watch video-taped movies. We talk with passengers and crew members and listen to taped music and radio, scanning the short wave bands for that precious commodity, an English language broadcast. We watch the sea and the stars. From the bow of the ship we delight in the flying fish sailing out of the way as the ship disturbs their own cruising, or dolphin playing chicken with the ship by jumping from one side to the other just in front of the bow slicing through the water at 18 knots. After dark the stars almost filling in the black sky on a clear night as viewed from the bridge roof provide many special moments in any voyage. Of course we always hope to see whales, but unless you spend long hours on the bridge watching the sea and the radar scope sighting whales is mostly a matter of luck. On this cruise we were lucky; two whales swam along the starboard side one sunny day in the Indian Ocean. Perhaps it is as illuminating to consider what we do not do while at sea. We don't battle automobile traffic; we don't live through rush hours, we rarely answer telephones, or struggle with problems which refuse to go away ashore, and we don't pack and unpack our suitcases repeatedly. In a word we are replenished, recharged, nourished. As we reported in chapter one an ocean voyage is recreation for us in the literal sense of that word.

The North Pacific in early April can be a bit unfriendly. By staying south of the minimal great circle route to Japan we kept some distance between us and the Aleutian low hovering to our north. We weren't able to escape altogether but we had hoped to take the worst of the winds and waves on our aft quarter rather than head on. For seven days the strategy worked to perfection. We had mild seas and even on days six and seven when the wind and seas were higher they were indeed on our aft quarter. Day eight was different. It was cold and blustery; winds were force eight on the Beaufort Scale which is defined as, "Gale. Moderately high waves of greater length; edges of crest begin to break into spindrift; foam is blown in well-marked streaks along the direction of the wind." By the next day the 35 knot winds had shifted and were coming at our starboard forward quarter. Asian Senator reduced her speed to 9.8 knots but still pitched heavily. There was surprisingly little roll but the spray from the bow crashing into a big wave rose at least 50 meters and washed over the entire ship back to the deck house. It is quite a sensation to stand in the wheelhouse five decks above the main deck and some 100 meters aft of the bow and see bow waves sheeting the glass right in front of you. Day ten was cloudy and rain fell from time to time but the wind was down and there were no white caps on the sea surrounding us. The rain helped wash the containers free of salt which had been deposited by the spray of the past two days. We had been able to walk on deck all but day nine when we settled for the exercise bike in the ship's gymnasium. Day twelve dawned sunny with the Japanese coast in sight and scores of small craft in view as well. We were given a revised expected docking time for Yokohama of 5:30 in the afternoon of the next day with a projected departure ten hours later. It looked like our useful shore leave would be very limited.

In addition to conversation at meals, from 10:30 until noon each Sunday was set aside for a happy hour for the captain, chief mate, chief engineer, and passengers. The other officers were invited but they rarely attended. The second mate had the morning watch and I'm not sure why the others didn't come. In any event the five passengers and the three senior officers typically were there. This is the same group which sat together at mealtime. The conversations were wide-ranging but often they evolved into a sort of cross-cultural comparison of the German way and the American way of doing things. We tended to get to such abstract topics by starting out with some item in the news or some comment based on what someone was reading or the video of some movie or what one of the Germans might say about his perception of America based upon his experience in a port and before long explanations precipitated comparisons and there we were. The Germans knew more about the United States than we knew about Germany. That was not surprising given their brush with American culture not only as Europeans whose entire lives had been lived in the shadow of American geopolitical and military action but also their role in the international business in which they were engaged. Further, they all had good to excellent command of the English language. So, while they suffered a bit from an over exposure to the pop cultural aspects of American society, they tended to know something about the United States at a deeper level. Nevertheless their understanding of American police and judicial jurisdictions, for example, was not only slim but remained skeptical. German political and social institutions are much more monolithic than ours and I think this resonates with the German personality better than the structurally messy way our multileveled approach has developed. They particularly had trouble reconciling county sheriffs as a part of our law enforcement constellation since sheriffs were elected and thus not necessarily professionally qualified officers. The German society places much emphasis on licensing and credentialing as a means of insuring competent practice, not just in the professions but throughout the occupational spectrum. And so our conversations carried on: explanation, justification, defense of the German (or the American) way, polite agreement to disagree, and, hopefully, increased insight into each other's alternatives and constraints on health care, unemployment benefits, immigration policy, German reunification, NATO, etc., etc. All five passengers remembered Hitler's Germany as children or young adults in the United States; none of the German officers did. The eldest of them was a very small boy at the close of World War II. And thus not only did we bring different national backgrounds to our roundtable but also differences implicit between those who had personal histories which predated 1945 and those who did not. One day the captain, who tended to be very sure about everything he had to say (not unlike most of the sea captains with whom we have sailed), was complaining about the expectations of the people of the former German Democratic Republic (East Germany). "They all expect good jobs that don't demand hard work, plenty of money, and birth to death security. They think that unification means a BMW, Japanese electronics, and American clothes for them all—and right away!" The discussion went on to bemoan the sorry state of East German factories, utilities, roads, and their economy in general and how big a drain on West German resources it will be to help East Germany advance to a point where their production of goods could be competitive in the global market. "It's a good thing," the captain said, "That Germany doesn't need to spend much of its wealth on its armed forces. After all," he continued, "America provides the security we need so we don't have to worry very much about the Balkans or Israel or other such places." There was a brief period of silence and then I said, "Well, captain, if Germany thinks it can continue as one of the economic giants of the world and, with the Japanese, enjoy bargain basement security at the expense of the United States in both dollars and blood then you and they have made a gross miscalculation. The American people are tired of seeing caskets delivered to Delaware or California with the remains of our young service men killed in the Middle East or the Balkans or anywhere else while nations which perpetrated World War II grow wealthier and complain about American fiscal irresponsibility and the need to rehabilitate East Germany. Who, after all, rehabilitated West Germany and Japan? Furthermore, Americans are not much interested in working as hired guns to insure the security of Europeans or Asians whose investment is devoted to developing even more wealth while others man the ramparts." The captain opened his mouth but elected not to respond. Vivian, the oldest passenger, quietly said, "I think you're right, Bob."

On balance, we learned more from our German ship's officers in our discussions than they did from us. That morning the reverse was true. The promise of freedom and prosperity which played an important role in the collapse of East Germany as soon as the USSR pulled out its support is almost sure to sustain reunified Germany as it pulls its eastern half up by its bootstraps. Abba Eban, the Israeli leader once remarked that men and nations adopt wise policies as soon as they have exhausted all other options. Surely this applies to Germany today. Throughout much of the first half of the twentieth century they exhausted all other options, including several that no one else would have dreamed possible. One lesson post-war Germans must learn and learn well is that even after half a century the past's legacy will not and should not disappear, not from the memories of those who remember at any rate. There is a clear difference between amnesty and amnesia. A striking parallel to all of this is the persistent set of indelible tensions and grievances which make it so hard for whites and blacks to live together in true psychic peace in America. If today's Germans have something to learn here, so do today's Americans.

At mid morning on the day we were to berth in Yokohama we shut down our engine and drifted about 25 miles outside the mouth of Tokyo Bay until 2:00 p.m. At 4 o'clock we picked up a bay pilot and began our passage up Tokyo Bay with scores of ships streaming past us on their way out. Helicopters and airplanes joined the chorus and about five o'clock we anchored off Yokohama's container port waiting for our harbor pilot until 6:00 and berthing at the Sealand Terminal at seven o'clock. The ship was cleared and we had our shore passes within 30 minutes. We walked to the terminal gate, went into an office building and asked one of the workers still at his desk to call a taxi for us which he did. We had decided to go to the Seamen's Club which we had been told was a short taxi ride of about ten minutes. It turned out to be even shorter, about one and one-half miles, but it still cost 1100 yen (about $9.00)! We bought postcards, looked around (there were video games, a bar and restaurant, a barber shop, gift shop, and currency exchange) and taxied back to the port gate. Unloading/ loading began at ten o'clock and six hours later we were on our way to Osaka with arrival projected for 7:30 a.m. the following day. We drifted for three hours in order to reach Osaka's pilot station at the scheduled hour and tied up at the dock at 7:25. Osaka has a large port situated around a gigantic harbor. There is much man-made acreage by virtue of landfill operations of startling magnitude. Our container terminal was on landfill, a large island actually, containing shopping, high-rise apartment and office buildings, a school, and a railroad station. After breakfast all five passengers went ashore walking to the shopping complex in the center of the island. We watched kindergarten classes engaged in calisthenics in their school playground and older adults playing croquet in a nearby park. We weren't able to venture further afield because we had only about three hours before being due back on board. At 1:45 we were underway bound for Pusan, Korea. The next morning we picked up a pilot for our passage between the Japanese islands of Hunshu and its southern neighbor Kyoshu through the Kanmon Strait. Due to the strength of the winds in the fairly narrow channel westbound ships had to pass through between 10:00 a.m. and 1:00 p.m. or wait for a later time slot. We dropped our pilot just before noon and headed across the Sea of Japan for the Korean peninsula.

By mid morning the next day we were cleared to go ashore in Pusan. After waiting in the anchorage in the early morning we moved into the harbor where 40 years ago the materials and personnel needed to wage war further north on the peninsula were unloaded. It was not hard to visualize this harbor in those days as we slowly approached the container terminal area. Bobby and I together with Vivian and Carol walked to the port gate, found a taxi, and rode to the railroad station plaza where we talked with the lady in the tourist information office. She had very little facility with English and we had no facility at all with Korean but we confirmed that the city tour we wanted would depart at 2:30 in the afternoon and that we could book it at another office about 50 yards away which was locked up! We changed money at a nearby bank and spent two hours shopping. We failed to find the yarn Bobby needed to finish a project even with an assist from a Korean shopkccpcr who took us down one narrow street after another. We met Carol and Vivian who had had quite an adventure in a nearby restaurant. Vivian had ordered lunch which she thought cost 3500 waan; in fact the price was 35,000 waan! About $46.00. She and Carol had a heated conversation with the restaurant people because Vivian was sure they had made a mistake on her tab. They finally added dollars to the waan they had all of which added up to about $40. At that point the restaurant manager said, "OK!" and Vivian and Carol escaped without having to wash dishes or explain themselves to the police. Pooling all our remaining Korean money we had enough for the tour tickets plus about 2000 waan which Bobby and I spent spliting a Wendy's hamburger. That's right! A Wendy's hamburger on the edge of the plaza in front of Pusan's railroad station. At 2 o'clock we returned to the tour kiosk where we learned that we four were the only customers for that afternoon's tour. The bus company had substituted a car and an English-speaking driver for the standard bus and Korean- speaking driver at no extra cost, not a bad deal at all. For the next three hours we toured the United Nations Memorial Cemetery, the beach front, and a magnificent Buddhist temple and monastery high above the coastal plain in the nearby mountains. The driver took us back to the port rather than the railroad station which we appreciated very much and by 5:45 we were in our staterooms. Asian Senator remained at her berth overnight, leaving for Kaoshiung, Taiwan, about a three day journey to the south, early in the morning.

Pusan had had very comfortable spring-like weather but as we sailed south to Taiwan the temperature and humidity both increased markedly. Kaoshiung is on the southern coast of Taiwan so we sailed the length of the island before anchoring to await berthing space. We remained at anchor for 32 hours before moving in to the dock at 10:00 p.m. Shore leave was posted as ending at 11 o'clock the next morning in preparation for a 12:30 departure for Hong Kong. The President Kennedy, a large container ship in the American President Line's fleet which we had seen in Oakland and in Yokohama, was also here. Before we left the President Hoover, another APL ship, came into the port. Hoover was a LASH ship which had been converted to strictly container cargo. A LASH ship is designed to load and unload barges from the aft end as well as carry containers as deck cargo. The deckhouse is forward rather than aft and, since it is positioned in front of the deck cargo, it is not as high as it would be on a typical container or general cargo ship. After breakfast we walked to the port gate and out to the road accessing the throughway which led to the city. Having less than three hours at best we opted not to spend the $40 required for a taxi to and from the city center. The port was a long distance from downtown Kaoshiung and there was no community close to the terminal gates so we walked along the access road with a view of the anchorage, a coast guard station, and not much else. We had a nice conversation with a man who worked for Evergreen, a major Taiwanese shipping company. He had been in 46 different countries and had lived in the United Kingdom for six years. He was concerned about the problems of pollution which faced Taiwan. Bobby asked him if his children were aware of such concerns and he said they were. She asked him if his parents were also concerned. He laughed and said his parents were only concerned about having enough to eat and a place to live. If having enough of the necessities meant polluting, so be it. He said he spent a good deal of time thinking about who he was and what he should be, topics his parents would regard as absurd. He seemed a bit unsympathetic to their points of view but I couldn't help thinking that if any of us had lived through the trauma of fleeing to Taiwan and scratching out a new life, a new opportunity, as had his parents' generation we might not be as concerned about environmental issues or "what is life" questions either. Misguided or shortsighted as it may be only a society which has established its security in a virile economic base is likely to regard environmental issues with any lasting fervor. A mother and father caught up in the daily struggle to feed, clothe, and house their family make decisions based on more immediate considerations. We finally left the dock at Kaoshiung in mid afternoon, delayed while the stevedore company tracked down our final two containers for loading and by a brief but violent thunder storm. Next port: Hong Kong.

Immediately after breakfast we went on deck to watch our entrance into Hong Kong. The container terminal was on the outskirts of Kowloon across the bay from Hong Kong. As we passed through the outer portion of this magnificent deep water harbor we saw that the surrounding hills were liberally laced with high-rise apartment buildings on the north and east sides. There were many ships in the channel both inbound and outbound. About half of our Filipino crew were leaving the ship today, going home after three 'round the world cruises in Asian Senator; they were excited and ready! Their replacements would

41

come on board this afternoon, including a new cook and a new steward. A few minutes before 10:00 we entered the inner harbor. The day was cloudy and haze obscured the shorelines but we moved steadily to the terminal berth and at 10:30 we were alongside. By the time everyone had eaten an early lunch, made purchases from the vendors who came aboard, and just plain moved out it was after noon. All five passengers left together and caught the port shuttle bus to the gate. We then set out to walk to the Mariner's Club to change some money. Vivian decided right away that walking was not a good thing for her to do so she found a taxi and was whisked off to downtown Kowloon's shops. The rest of us proceeded to the subway station about a quarter mile beyond the club. We got off the subway train in downtown Kowloon, looked for yarn, walked to the Star Ferry dock and purchased tickets for a 3:00 tram tour of Hong Kong's streets. We four plus three women from Australia comprised the tour group shepherded by a young Hong Kong woman. We crossed on the ferry to Hong Kong, boarded a private double decker bus (open top deck) and rode to the tram barn where we boarded one of the three original trams built around 1903 for a ride through the streets of central Hong Kong. Their trams are double decker street cars which still provide much of the downtown public transportation. We were served soft drinks, peanuts, gimsum (sort of Chinese tea including shrimp roll, meat pastries, vegetable and bean dishes, and tea) as we rolled through the streets. Our specially outfitted tram had red velvet upholstery throughout; it was quite elegant with its polished wood and brass fittings. Shortly after 5 o'clock we were back on the Kowloon side of the harbor and a few minutes later we were in a taxi racing (whenever possible) through the rush hour traffic which included pedestrians who competed for street space with the vehicles. Neither side, walkers or drivers, were inclined to yield and on two occasions we were sure our taxi was going to run down a pedestrian. Mayhem was avoided at the last possible instant and by six o'clock we were back to the sanctuary of Asian Senator. Loading continued until 1:00 a.m. and we left

Hong Kong bound for Singapore at three in the morning. Our hope was to do a lot more exploring and walking around than we had been able to accomplish in the Asian ports so far; we vowed to do better in Singapore.

The weather had become sunny and hot; the moderating sea breeze continued to keep the deck comfortable but care had to be taken to avoid too much tropical sun. The ship's air conditioning system was running full force. After all, the deckhouse was a steel box in the sun on top of an engine room with an exhaust stack running through it! The bosun and his crew washed down the entire deckhouse in preparation for a lot of chipping and painting between now and our arrival in Europe. There were nine decks in the deckhouse not including the various levels in the engine room. Starting at the bottom there was the upper deck which included the ship's office with computer, ballast control board, etc., the stevedore's room, and a gymnasium. The upper deck was Asian Senator's main deck and stretched from stem to stern. The remaining decks were only in the deckhouse itself with the exception of the poop deck. Inside, the poop deck contained the galley, dining rooms, lounges for both crew and officers and passengers, and the hospital. Outside aft of the deckhouse, the poop deck roofed the upper deck and had containers stacked on it. The crew deck housed the crew. The boat deck contained cabins for officers, the swimming pool, and the life boats. The supernumerary deck had two double staterooms for passengers. The chief's deck had a single passenger stateroom plus the quarters for the chief engineer. The captain's deck contained the captain's suite and a cabin for the radio officer. The navigation deck housed the bridge and bridge wings plus chart and communication rooms. And finally the bridge roof was an open deck above the navigation deck.

The day we were to arrive in Singapore our schedule was modified. Rather than meeting the pilot at 1:00 p.m. and docking about two o'clock, we were to be at the pilot station at 5:30 p.m. docking one hour later. The first hint of this change came at mid morning when Asian Senator turned off course by some 90° and shut down her engine. We thought we were ahead of schedule but at lunch the change was announced. Since we were expecting to be docked a total of about ten hours the 6:30 arrival left only the possibility of shopping (dependent on store hours) and perhaps a meal ashore. Darkness comes by 7 o'clock in the tropics so sight seeing and walking through the market streets were out the window. The pilot came aboard at 5:30 but our berth was not yet available. We finally docked at 7:30 and it was another half hour before the gangway was down and our passports were issued. It was raining lightly: 100% humidity and 90° Fahrenheit! There was no breeze of any consequence. Carol, Bobby, and I went ashore taking the port shuttle bus to the gate. We walked about three or four blocks to the Amana Hotel's shopping arcade where two shops and a currency exchange were still open. Most of the stores had closed at 5:30. We bought a few items, mainly snacks and sundries, and then walked through the neighboring streets for a few minutes before returning to the port and our ship about 10:30. We watched the gantry cranes at work unloading and loading containers for half an hour and then showered and went to bed. Oh, we did one final chore before calling it a day. We secreted most of our money, half of our traveler's checks, and Bobby's jewelry. Upon leaving Singapore we were to sail through the Strait of Malacca which is notorious for its pirates. That's right, pirates! There are just a handful of places along the world's trade routes where pirates operate and the Strait of Mallaca with the Indonesian archipelago forming its southern boundary was a notorious one. Our captain had been robbed by pirates on an earlier passage and he was alert to the danger. Apparently the Indonesian authorities did not patrol their coast rigorously and high speed pirate boats have overtaken a fair number of ships in the strait. Since all traffic between Singapore and Suez uses this route there were always plenty of targets. On the navigation bridge there was a notice posted giving the call numbers of several naval and coast guard services to contact in case a pirate craft was observed. When we awoke at 6:30 a.m.

we were well away from Singapore and in the Strait of Malacca for the next 30 hours. We passed the northwestern tip of Sumatra on our port side and entered the Indian Ocean without spotting any pirates. I'm sure that was one experience worth missing.

Asian Senator's roll increased from virtually none to an amplitude of 20°-25°; not severe at all, but quite a contrast to the waters of the strait. There were no white caps but the long ocean swells were moving from south to north. The southern seas are pretty substantial at that time of year; the swells were coming straight from the vast southern ocean unimpeded by any appreciable land mass between Antarctica and the Indian subcontinent. Our course was to be past the southern tip of Sri Lanka and straight to the mouth of the Red Sea, about a ten day passage.

We were some five weeks into our 12 week circum-navigation and were getting more familiar with the officers and crew, especially the three senior officers with whom we ate our meals. In talking with them it became clear that the German Merchant Navy had troubles which were not very different from those of the United States Merchant Marine. In the simplest terms crews composed of seamen from countries like Germany and the United States were being forced out of the market by lower priced seamen from less affluent societies. In the United States, where the maritime unions had a complete lock on all jobs, this phenomenon was manifest in a shrinking merchant marine whose remaining elements stay afloat only through government contracts and subsidies justified in terms of the national security needs for a viable merchant fleet. Thus the amount of work for American crews is dwindling to an alarmingly low level. In Germany it is possible to hire largely foreign crews (Asian Senator had eight Germans in a crew of 22) and thus the amount of work for German seamen is also dwindling. The result among our highly competent German officers seemed to be a serious deterioration in morale. They did not seem to have confidence in the potential and performance of their international crewmen and they worried about the lack of opportunity for young Germans who would like to be seamen. They performed excellently as ship's officers but one sensed they did this because of pride in their competence and the responsibility they assume rather than confidence that what they do will lead to a secure and flourishing future. They feel the hot breath of cheaper workers who are filling a greater and greater proportion of the available berths in the German fleet and who ultimately may overwhelm German seamen, perhaps even themselves. One beautiful evening as we headed west through the Indian Ocean the evening meal was turned into a barbecue for the entire ship's company held on the port boat deck. There were beer, wine, and soft drinks; sausages, pork chops; potato salad and vegetables. The Filipino crewmen played guitars and sang. There were strings of colored lights and the flags of three nations: Germany, the Philippines, and the United States. Everyone clapped but only the Filipinos sang. Having the party was surely a good thing to do but the cultural barriers in place for an array of reasons did not really lower perceptibly.

News of the acquittal of all four Los Angeles policemen on trial for beating Rodney King who had been arrested for several moving vehicle violations including resisting arrest came over the short wave radio. And hard on the heels of this unexpected result, news of rioting in Los Angeles as well as several other cities came through. Of course the news itself was very bad but I include it in this narrative because it led to a long explanation of the role and control of the National Guard in the United States. Trying to first explain and then rationalize the organization of our National Guard to people who are not familiar with the myriad ways in which political power is portioned out and balanced in America is a non-trivial task. For example, from our German friends: "You mean the governor of one of your states can activate units of your National Guard even though it is a part of the nation's military reserve? How can that be allowed? How can the National Guard be responsible to both a governor and the president?" One of the most enlightening aspects of being with our German officers was the on-going dialogue about life and customs in our respective homes. We were, I believe, most surprised to learn that the officers regarded their country as economically less able than the United States. Particularly with the advent of reunification they saw a long period of tough times for Germany. We told them that little of what worried them so profoundly had found its way into the American press and thus Americans picture Germany as having gigantic economic strength. They talked again about the miserable state of industrial infrastructure in the former East Germany. As they saw it East German industry was totally unable to compete in the world market and required a complete overhaul. Not only was the infrastructure sick but the people assumed (our West Germans said) that the government owed them a job, security, health care, a funded retirement, and not much hard work. How long it will take to turn all of Germany into the economic success demonstrated in the west is hard to say. Perhaps truth and correct forecasting lie somewhere between our ship's officers' fears and America's lack of insight. In any event, their repeated references to what faces unified Germany were both revealing and sobering.

As we approached the Gulf of Aden on our last day in the Indian Ocean we picked up a Christian Science Monitor Radio report on the presence of a shipload of grain about to be unloaded in civil warring Somalia in the port of Boosaaso. There was concern about whether unloading would be accomplished without incident. The most optimistic commentator, a food relief administrator, said he expected to unload successfully but held out no hope that peaceful distribution of the grain could be made in that famished society. He said it would require several shiploads unloaded before the frenzy to get some of the precious food would moderate. It seems hard to believe that the plenty of our ship's larder cruised right by this kind of misery. There are certainly great distances in just a few miles. After ten days on the Indian Ocean we entered the Gulf of Aden, passing through the Strait of Bab al Mendob with the tiny nation of Djibouti harboring a French navel base on the African side nestled between Somalia and Ethiopia. To starboard was the Arabian Peninsula, more particularly, Yemen. Until recently there were two Yemens: North and South. One was a protégé of China; the other of the Soviet Union. They were joined a few years ago into a single socialist nation.

There was what appeared to be a perpetual haze which limited visibility to a few miles but it wasn't really haze at all. It was sand, minute particles of sand in the air, everywhere. Bone dry desert east and west together with enough wind to suspend some sand particles in the atmosphere created enough airborne material to induce that silica haze. Was it enough to precipitate lung disease among those who lived there? I do not know, but there was enough to coat Asian Senator and her containers with a sandy dust. And there was enough to limit visibility in otherwise clear weather. About half way up the Red Sea we drifted all day long as the chief engineer and his crew pulled a piston, changed its rings, and cleaned its cylinder's valves. Once each circumnavigation a piston and its cylinder are overhauled so in seven voyages the entire engine is rebuilt. Late in the afternoon the captain, chief mate, and chief engineer were lowered in the inflatable life raft and took a spin around our drifting ship. When they returned, the captain asked me if I would like to go out in the inflatable. "Absolutely," I responded. We climbed over the rail of the crew deck into the raft and were lowered to the sea by one of our small cranes. Releasing the crane's hook we fired up the outboard motor and planed across the swells heading away from Asian Senator for about a half mile. We then circled the ship taking a close look at her hull, rudder, and propeller as we went around. The jelly fish which were in great numbers along the shady side of the ship looked more or less white from the decks; close up from the raft they were many different and delicate pastel shades. Beautiful to look at; not so beautiful to swim among! Three days earlier four of the five passengers had participated fully in a life boat drill which included wearing life jackets and helmets, lowering the boats with all of us aboard and both seat and shoulder belts fastened, and cruising in the sea for about 15 minutes before returning to the ship and being hoisted on board. Asian Senator's life boats were wonderful pieces of equipment designed so that even if capsized they would right themselves. In the northern oceans such boats reduce exposure to the sun, wind, and water to endurable limits. They perform the same functions in tropical climates but they are hot! I lost an amazing amount of moisture through perspiration

48

during that 20 minute ride; my shoes were soaked through from perspiration running down my legs. Several of the crew and passengers suffered motion sickness. Even a smooth appearing sea is not so quiet that a lifeboat doesn't pitch and roll. Doing this in an enclosed and hot environment makes the sensations that much worse. If I were forced to abandon ship I would certainly choose the greater protection of an enclosed boat but for a joyride in the Red Sea the inflatable was far superior.

We made good progress up the Red Sea and were somewhat ahead of our schedule for transiting the Suez Canal so the captain elected to spend some additional time drifting rather than going directly to the anchorage at Suez to await our designated north-bound convoy to Port Said and the Mediterranean. Much of the time visibility was limited to about three miles due to the sand particles in the air. On Mothers' Day (as celebrated in the United States) we approached the anchorage at Suez prior to transiting the canal the next day. We gave some seven-up to the other two mothers on board to mark their day. That evening the pilot came on board and we moved to our position in the inner harbor to await the formation of the northbound convoy in the morning.

Asian Senator in the Red Sea.

At seven o'clock we were underway behind an Evergreen container ship and in front of a K-Line ship. We had six Egyptians plus their small boat on board. In case we had to tie up during the transit they would handle the lines. They practiced their secondary vocation (or was it primary?): selling Egyptian goods to passengers and crew throughout the day. There is a fair amount of irrigation from the waters of the Nile River along the lower half of the canal. But by afternoon both shores were sand, sand, and more sand. The highway from Suez to Port Said paralleled the canal on the west bank and, from time to time, roads radiated from the east bank ferry ramps across the Sinai Peninsula toward Israel. The entire length of the canal was dotted by military installations along the west bank, in part vestiges from the days when Israel occupied the Sinai. In Ismaillya, the only large city along the canal between Suez and Port Said, we sailed past the Egyptian president's villa overlooking the waterway. We took the new channel which passes about two or three miles east of Port Said and shortly after dinner we dropped our pilot and line handlers/merchants and were in the Mediterranean Sea bound for the Strait of Gibraltar.

The second day in the Mediterranean we drifted for two hours to enable the engineers to grind an exhaust valve. Then we resumed at full speed because we had been rescheduled to arrive in Rotterdam, our first European port, twelve hours earlier than originally posted. At 85% of full power which is regarded as our upper limit Asian Senator's speed was 19.5 knots and doors and light fixtures tended to rattle a bit. We passed the Rock of Gibraltar at four o'clock on a hazy early morning and by breakfast we were well beyond the strait with Rotterdam scheduled for late evening in three days. The Atlantic was relatively quiet with breezes, occasionally some white caps, but nothing to prevent us from scurrying along at 19.5 knots. The chief mate told me when we came into the English Chanel but there was enough haze to make it seem like the open ocean: no land in sight. We had a stiff breeze all day but it was cooler, about 14° Celsius at breakfast time. There had been a further revision of our schedule; we were supposed to pick up the Rotterdam pilot at noon and dock at 3:15 p.m.. It looked like shore leave in Rotterdam would be late afternoon and evening. The pilot actually joined us at 11:30, we docked at 2:30, and by 3:00 we were cleared for shore and Bobby and I walked to the nearest port gate, then into the village of Pernis, a total walk of about 20 minutes. We changed money, shopped at a supermarket, walked the streets of this lovely town of row houses, lawns, and gardens and then took a bus to Zud Plein, a shopping, transportation, commercial, and residential center just across the river from downtown Rotterdam. Almost all the Zud Plein stores closed at 5:30 but we found a restaurant and ordered cold plates for supper. After our meal we went to a McDonalds in the shopping mall for sundaes and coffee. (There is something to that old saw that you can take the boy out of the country, but not the country out of the boy, I guess!) We spent our final 6.5 guilders on bus fare back to Euro Container Terminal and watched the ETC gantry cranes and crews unload and load containers for an hour. We had begun the five port marathon which was Asian Senator's European itinerary. The schedule of arriving at Bremmerhaven at ten o'clock the next evening had been revised to a 7:30 arrival. Later word was received that dock space at Bremmerhaven would be available even earlier. Just like any other homing organism we headed for the only German port on the itinerary at 19.5 knots, docking at 6:00 p.m.. The chief engineer's wife came on board and into the dining room before we had finished dinner. A school teacher, she had taught until 1:30, picked up a large supply of bread for the ship at her local bakery (it was great bread!), packed and drove 75 kilometers to the port. An hour later we met the wife of the captain (who came from southern Germany to welcome her husband home for his vacation), and the wife of our chief mate who lived about 60 kilometers away. It was to have been the start of his vacation also but he had been offered the captaincy of Asian Senator and had decided to accept thereby postponing his vacation for another three months. We went to the port gate but could not find any place to change money and decided to wait until morning to go into the city. By 9:00 a.m. we had taken city buses into Bremmerhaven's center, had changed money, and begun the shopping we had planned. We also spent about two hours in a large nautical museum. We were to be back on board by one o'clock and so we were ready to find our bus stop when we ran into Bob and Carol. They told us that shore leave had been extended until four o'clock! Good news, but not knowing about the change until midday was unfortunate. Nevertheless, the extra time was really welcome. We bought some fruit and rolls and found a bench overlooking the river front near a beach area. Some young men were playing with an American football. Two of them had some idea of how to throw a pass and two of them didn't have a clue. Bobby swears the beach was optionally topless. I took her word for it; whatever evidence there had been to buttress her assertion was missed by me, worse luck. After lunch we walked through a Lutheran churchyard (the church itself was locked) and the residential neighborhood adjacent to the shopping street before bussing back to the container port. Rather than wait 50 minutes for the bus which would have taken us to our gate we took another bus whose driver said he could drop us only a short walk from our gate. It wasn't a bad walk but it wasn't a short one. We arrived at the ship at 3:45. The loading continued until 5:30 and an hour later we left bound for Felixstowe, a small resort city and major port in southeastern England. In early afternoon the next day we docked at Felixstowe. Coming into the harbor the pilot pointed out three small ships also on their way into port. They were vessels that had participated in the Dunkerque evacuation of the British army in 1940. A regatta involving these old craft was scheduled for the next day. It was hard to realize that that evacuation had taken place over half a century earlier, before the pilot had been born. Sailing those waters on a German ship and seeing those old vessels shined up with pennants flying was a rather sobering event. By two o'clock we were cleared by British immigration and on our way by van to the Seamen's Mission at the port gate.

Our van driver was one of the clergymen assigned to the mission and he gave us good information about Felixstowe and the bus service available as well as a street map to help us find our way. Bobby and I elected to walk into town, only about four kilometers from the mission. We walked along the beach front street which sported all the usual beach resort attractions from an amusement park to salt water taffy to tacky T-shirts. We were ahead of the summer season even though the spring afternoon was quite warm so we saw mostly retired people along the walks, sort of a British version of the St. Petersburg, Florida stereotype. We walked for a fair distance past the town center along the beach and finally turned up the bluffs and back through a residential neighborhood to the town center. About five o'clock we ran into Carol and the three of us went into a tiny pizza parlor run by a Turk for salad and pizza; the food was good. By eight o'clock we were back on board Asian Senator. While in town we had talked to a delightful little old lady who came up to us because she had noticed us walking around the neighborhood and thought we were lost. Perhaps that was just an excuse to find out who the strangers were. In any case she was charming and we were glad she had stopped us. We also talked at some length with a couple who were working in their garden as we walked along their street. Bobby asked them the name of a particular flowering tree we had seen in the Netherlands and in Felixstowe and that led to an extended conversation. It was really nice to make these personal contacts; we remember them best of all whenever we recall our day in Felixstowe.

Late the next morning we were in the ship channel and then entered the mouth of the river which led to Antwerp, Belgium. By 2:30 p.m. we were berthed at a container terminal some 14 miles from the center of the city. Bob, Carol, Bobby and I left the ship by taxi at four o'clock to spend the next five hours in town. It was a Saturday and stores were open until 5:30. The streets were filled with people and vehicles and the sidewalk cafes were filling in rapidly. The sun was shining in a cloudless sky; it was a lovely spring day. Bobby and I walked from the

Central Railroad Station toward and then through the principal shopping street which had been converted into a gigantic pedestrian mall. Then turning toward the river front we visited the main cathedral where a service was in progress. At 6:00 p.m. we were walking along the river walk past the maritime museum, river cruise boats, refreshment kiosks, and scores of families out for a late afternoon stroll. To be more accurate, the parents were strolling; the children were generally moving at somewhat higher velocities. We curved back into the city streets moving in what we believed to be the general direction of the Central Station. Stopping to eat at a Belgium fast food emporium which had outdoor tables, we had a passable shrimp salad. We ambled through a large park with curving paths, waterways, and a number of statues quite near the city center. There was a large gathering of families in the park who appeared to be orthodox Jews. Everyone was dressed up: the men in dark suits, the women in dresses, not sports clothing at all, and the children's attire was clearly more appropriate for synagogue than the grass of the park. On the way back to Central Station to meet our taxi we walked down a street devoted almost entirely to gold, silver, and diamond merchants, one of Antwerp's leading businesses. Shortly after 10 p.m. we were back on board Asian Senator and learned that the threat of a dock strike in Le Havre had caused us to scratch that port from our itinerary so we were going from Antwerp directly to New York harbor and Port Elizabeth, New Jersey. At 2:30 a.m. we were underway; it had been eight weeks since boarding at Long Beach and in ten days we would see the Statue of Liberty upon our return to United States waters.

Weather forecasts called for a low pressure cell in the Atlantic which caused us to alter the normal great circle route to New York. The new plan called for us to head directly to 50°N/30°W from the southwest corner of Ireland, then directly to 40°N/47°W. From that point we were to head almost directly west into New York. Our route, which looked something like the sketch below, was longer than the great circle route but was designed to escape the worst of the low pressure area by first heading north of the great circle path and then, by dropping south to 40° north latitude to avoid that part of the Atlantic where icebergs might be encountered. Canceling the Le Havre stop provided ample time for the extra distances involved. The plan worked beautifully. Our heaviest weather came in the eastern

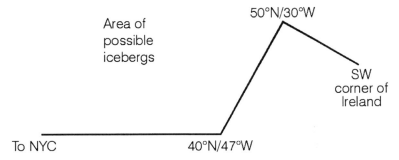

Atlantic on the way to 50°N/30°W. The high pressure area over Europe had stopped the forward progress of the Atlantic low and pressures slowly rose over the ocean. We had two days of noticeable rolling and pitching in Force 5 and 6 winds but the winds were on our stern quarter rather than in our teeth and by the third day we were down to Force 3 and 4 winds. After that the Atlantic acted like a pussycat. The big event of our Atlantic crossing was Bobby's haircut provided by our Filipino radio officer! I continued to get bushier and bushier.

It was pretty easy to determine when Asian Senator was in the Gulf Stream as we made our way through the western Atlantic Ocean. One day the water temperature was 13° Celsius (55° F); the next day it was 21.5° C (71° F)! What a contrast. The Gulf Stream, one of the great ocean currents of the world, moderates the climate of North America's eastern seaboard as well as the climate of the United Kingdom and Western Europe. Asian Senator routinely measures sea and air temperatures, wind velocity and direction, dew point, humidity, and barometric pressure. Worldwide, vessels at sea transmit about 100,000 weather reports per month to the various national programs throughout the globe. For example, the United States Voluntary Observing Ships (VOS) program receives meteorological data from over 1400 ships. Only the former USSR with close to 1700 reporting ships exceeded this total in 1990. Nations do not limit reporting to ships under their flags and all these reports are consolidated through the coordination of the World Meteorological Organization (WMO).

In spite of our longer routing from Europe to North America the cancellation of our Le Havre call led to two ten-hour periods of drifting so that we would arrive at the New York harbor pilot station at the scheduled time. The work of the ship went on, of course. The bosun devoted much of the drifting time to painting the hull of the ship. Scaffolding was lowered over the side, a life ring was floated in the sea below, and the painters wore life jackets and safety belts as Asian Senator's blue coat was renewed. Chipping and painting are never-ending jobs on ocean ships. The chemical action of salt water on paint and steel must be constantly battled to keep the ship in good shape. The crew of Asian Senator spreads about five metric tons of paint on her surfaces each year!

At last the drifting was over; we moved steadily westward toward our landfall. We abandoned short-wave radio bands in favor of AM and FM transmissions from New England and then New York. At 3:30 a.m. on a June morning we picked up our New York pilots and by 5:00 we had passed under the Verrazano Bridge and were making a hard turn to port around the north end of Staten Island heading for the cargo ports of New Jersey. The Statue of Liberty was in view to the north as were the towers of Manhattan. We cruised past Bayonne on the starboard side of the channel and then, passing under the Bayonne Bridge, made a very sharp turn to starboard into Newark Bay. We docked between the cities of Elizabeth and Newark at the Port Elizabeth Container Terminal at 6:00 a.m.. By 7:15 we were cleared by United States Immigration and had our passports in hand. "Welcome home," smiled the immigration officer. I smiled back. For all the joys of this cargo ship cruise it was good to hear those words. We had been talking to one of the pilots about transportation from the terminal. He confirmed the advance information we had; it wasn't good. The pilot said he once told a taxi driver that he would walk to the port on his knees before paying the quoted fare! We were at Port Elizabeth for the entire day so we decided not to let the expense deprive us of a day in the city. And so we began our three port excursion along the eastern seaboard of the United States. After a very pleasant day ashore in New Jersey and Manhattan we returned to our ship in the early evening. We sailed at six o'clock the next morning reversing our path down Newark Bay, around the sharp turn at the south end of Bayonne, into the Kill Van Kull which separates New Jersey from Staten Island, then into lower New York Harbor, beneath the Verrazano Bridge, and out the Ambrose Light Channel. The cruise to Norfolk, Virginia, our second port of call on this coast, took one day. We drifted for three hours in order to meet our scheduled arrival at the pilot station off Chesapeake Bay at 3:00 a.m. We were tied up at our dock in Portsmouth's container terminal by 5:30. The pilot told us that we had arrived on the first day of a three day festival and that the kick off activity was to be a parade of ships, including several tall ships, which would pass right by our berth on its way to the waterfronts of downtown Norfolk and Portsmouth. The two cities lie across the river from each other and their waterfronts were about three miles upstream from our berth. We elected to stay on board to watch the parade of ships scheduled to arrive at its destination at noon. At 11:15 the parade's lead ship, a small navel vessel festooned with pennants, passed Asian Senator. We continued to watch the scores of sailboats, launches, and four tall ships passing in review through the first half of our lunch hour. We spent the afternoon shopping: our first K-Mart, Sears, Wall Mart and enclosed shopping mall complete with a frozen custard emporium since leaving California in the dimly recalled days of early spring. At 9:45 p.m. Asian Senator left bound for Savannah, Georgia. Bobby and I stayed on deck as we made our way down the channel toward the mouth of Chesapeake Bay. We wanted to have a waterfront view of Norfolk's Navel Base. It was here that the United States Atlantic Fleet was headquartered and, as a special treat for those of us on Asian Senator, three major US aircraft carriers were berthed side by side. Our pilot told us that this was the first time in over 40 years that three such carriers had been collected in one spot. Moreover, the plan was to have five major aircraft carriers at berth on July 4th. I believe that this was objective evidence that the cold war was definitely over, at least in the minds of the United States Navy and its Pentagon overseers.

The run to Savannah required a total of 35 ½ hours. We sailed past its beautifully restored waterfront along the Savannah River early on a Sunday morning and tied up at the container terminal about four miles further upstream shortly after nine o'clock. Our day ashore was split among the city's Visitors' Center and Museum; the historic district replete with beautiful old homes, churches, and monuments; and the river front plaza where old cotton warehouses have been converted into shops, restaurants, and cafes. That evening we watched the Chicago Bulls and the Portland Trailblazers on the ship's TV as they played game three of the NBA Championship Series. Just before the end of the game Asian Senator headed downstream to the Atlantic, the Caribbean, and Cristobal, the port at Colon, Panama, our next stop just prior to transiting the Panama Canal. I decided to stay up for the entire river passage under the high bridge carrying US 17 from South Carolina to Georgia, past the paper mills and pottery clay processing plant, down the winding channel with the green buoy lights winking off the starboard side and the red ones to port. Past the Georgia islands in the Savannah delta and further away to the north across the bay Hilton Head, South Carolina's premier resort mecca, and finally past the lighthouse on Tybee Island, Georgia's northernmost barrier island and into the Atlantic Ocean. The night was dark, the waters darker still except for the shimmer reflected off Asian Senator's lights aft of the navigation bridge. The breeze was fresh given our 18 knot velocity as the ship shouldered into her natural setting, the long rolls of the ocean swells. It was time for bed.

The route to Panama took us east of the Bahamas, past San Salvador, first western hemisphere landfall of Columbus, through the Windward Passage separating Cuba from Haiti, and down to Cristobal. The final three days of this leg were made at our 19.5 knot top cruising speed. The reason for our hurry was that once again a modest change in schedule had been directed by Senator Linie's operations office in New York. We had been asked to arrive at 1:00 p.m. rather than late in the evening. The captain signaled back that our best speed would put us at the pilot station at 1:45 p.m. We may go right in to the dock; we may not. Cristobal had space for only one large container ship and only one gantry crane was in working condition. Their second gantry had been out of commission for several months! When we arrived at the pilot station close to the harbor breakwater we started right in to the docks. As we moved slowly through the harbor and then waited for the tug boats we needed to dock we could see a large container ship coming down the channel exiting the Panama Canal. As we approached the dock we were surprised to see that the ship coming out of the canal was also a Senator Linie ship. As it turned out we had won a race. If the other ship had arrived before us we would have anchored waiting for it to unload and load. We stayed at the dock from Thursday afternoon until five o'clock Saturday morning, our reserved time for transiting the canal. We spent time in the duty free zone of Colon on Friday stopping at a super market on the way back to the ship. It was not a good day for Americans to be wandering around Panama. President Bush, who had stopped at Panama City on his way to Brazil, was unable to speak due to demonstrations and the resulting tear gassing of the crowd. The day before an American's automobile was bombed in Panama. US military personnel, government workers, and their families were cautioned to stay on US bases. There was a 9:00 p.m. curfew in effect for these people. All of this coupled with the fairly high probability of mugging in Colon put a damper on our natural inclination to walk through the neighborhoods.

By six o'clock Saturday we were in the channel southbound through the Panama Canal. Since people think of the canal as joining the Atlantic and Pacific Oceans (a correct understanding) many are led to two incorrect correlates: (1) the canal runs from east to west (it doesn't) and (2) passing from the Atlantic side to the Pacific side leaves you west of where you started (not true)! Colon is north and a bit west of Balboa, the city at the Pacific end of the canal. So traffic is referred to as northbound or southbound and Asian Senator was east of its 6 a.m. starting point upon exiting the canal at Balboa. To make things seem even more improbable, ships exiting the canal at Balboa and headed to northern ports such as those in the United States sail south for several hours before turning west and later northwest. Hard to believe? Examine a map of the Western Hemisphere and you will see that all of these improbables are true. Soon the United States will pull out of the operation of the Panama Canal all together. Until then Panama and the United States are operating the canal together with ever increasing authority and allocation of personnel falling upon Panama. We had two pilots, one about-to-retire American and a younger Panamanian. All the line handlers and donkey engine drivers were Panamanian. It was our first transit in ten years. The only difference we noticed was a far greater amount of debris on the lock decks this time. I asked our captain about that and he said he saw the same thing. He was not confident that the canal will be well maintained over the years. He cited the months of down time of one of the two gantry cranes at Cristobal as evidence. I hope he is worrying without cause; I suppose just about everyone shares that hope. Egypt has certainly been successful in operating the Suez Canal; why shouldn't Panama make a go of their canal? No doubt the relatively unstable governments and economies in Central America make many nervous about this vital seaway's future and a canal dependent on the smooth operation of three sets of locks is more mechanically demanding than a sea level passage such as Suez. In any event, the die is cast; the clock is running, and before long it will all be up to

Panama. Our passage was very efficient. From entry at 6 a.m. to exit at 2:30 p.m. Asian Senator had no delays or waits whatsoever. We didn't even pause in Gaton Lake which is a common occurrence in transiting. The average passage requires about 23 hours all told. We made it through in less than nine hours.

At this point we were on the last lap. We had boarded Asian Senator on March 29 in Long Beach; we expected to return to Long Beach docking early in the morning on June 20. The swimming pool was filled with warm Pacific seawater; the decks were washed down to rid us of the dirt from the container port in Cristobal, and we passengers began the process of reentry which always signals the forthcoming end of a long ocean cruise. All of us, crew and passengers, enjoyed a great barbecue on the boat deck one warm tropical evening. There was grilled meat and potato salad and everything else needed. There was beer and wine and singing and dancing. Beginning two days before reaching Long Beach there were suitcases and packing and customs declaration forms. The weather remained wonderful, moderating from the tropical heat of Panama as we made our way up the coast of Central America and Mexico. Our twelve week odyssey was ending. It was just about time to bid farewell to the containers!

What can we tell you in summary? Do we recommend a voyage as a passenger on a container ship? Well, sure we do, but with some stipulations and reservations. From the passenger's perspective the big difference between being on a container ship and being on a break-bulk ship or a bulk carrier is the amount of port time. Not counting our two calls at Long Beach where we embarked and disembarked, we were in 15 ports for a total of 241 hours. But of that time a certain amount was used to clear through customs and immigration formalities so that we could go ashore and then shore leave ended from one to five hours before actual departure. Subtracting those hours left 189 hours of shore leave throughout the twelve week voyage. Of those 189 hours, 116 hours were during daylight and thus more appropriate for sight seeing, touring, and the like. Of the 15 ports of call two, Yokohama and Singapore, provided no daylight hours of shore leave. Kaoshiung, with daylight shore leave ending at 11 a.m. and with the container port at great distance from the city's center provided very little shore side opportunity. Container terminals are often at significant distances from the cities they serve. They are generally newer than the other docking facilities and they require a lot of space to store and handle containers, ergo they tend to be further out. The bottom line goes something like this: if time ashore is as important to you as time at sea, if spending time in the ports of call is your principal reason for going, then be prepared to be somewhat disappointed with your container ship cruise. If you want the change of pace which a long sea voyage can induce, and if you regard significant shore time as a welcome but not crucial aspect of your cruise, then a container ship will be perfect for you. Most of us fall somewhere between such poles of interests and preferences. You must think carefully about yourself in this regard.

There are ways to modify your itinerary to suit your disposition. For example, we could have left Asian Senator in Rotterdam and rejoined her at Antwerp forgoing the cruises to Bremmerhaven, Felixstowe, and Antwerp. This would have given us several days in Europe to spend ashore as we saw fit. The same thing could have been done in Japan and on the eastern seaboard of the United States. Another way to influence the length of port time you might anticipate is to choose an itinerary which includes ports which tend to handle cargo less efficiently than is done in western Europe, the industrialized Far East, and the United States. For example, many people in a position to know would suggest that Latin America, the Caribbean, India, and Africa tend to have less high speed cargo handling in their container terminals. Still another strategy is to go on one ship, lay over at an appropriate port, and return on another vessel in the same liner service. All of these strategies are applicable and you should consider one or more of them if the voyage you want looks as though it might not generate enough shore time to make you content.

Container shipment is the primary mode of the present and will remain so in the future for intercontinental cargo. There will always be bulk carriers and specialty ships of various kinds but very few of these ships offer space to passengers. Break-bulk or general cargo ships are becoming more and more rare but there are still some available as you will learn when you read the next chapter.

3

ARE FREIGHTERS FOR YOU?

We think cruising in freighters is great; it is our dish of tea, but we realize cargo ships aren't for everyone. If you have a two or three week vacation which begins and ends on dates specified well in advance then there is no realistic way to arrange a cargo ship holiday. For one thing virtually all freighter voyages last longer than two or three weeks. And while you might consider a one way Atlantic crossing from Montreal or one of the eastern ports of the United States within a two week time frame, the degree of uncertainty of your exact embarkation date is a significant deterrent. Just a short delay past the forecast date would be enough to derail your vacation plans. Cargo is king in freighter scheduling and your embarkation date could be changed more than once before you board your ship to claim your stateroom. Container ships in long distance intercontinental liner service tend to adhere more closely to projected schedules but almost none of them have itineraries which would accommodate a short cruise of two weeks or so except for some one way trips and shorter segments. There are exceptions; for example, one ship which sails to South America carries up to 100 passengers in addition to its cargo and maintains a schedule much like that of a cruise ship. It accepts reservations for segments of its complete itinerary and offers air/sea packages which allow you to enjoy a week or two or three, flying either to join the ship, or home after leaving the ship, or both. While this ship carries cargo, it is really a hybrid, as much a cruise ship which carries freight as it is a freighter which carries passengers. It has an organized program of activities for passengers as is offered on any cruise ship. But let's say that your schedule is more flexible, that you have the time, and thus could seriously consider booking a freighter voyage. The question of whether you would be happy cruising with cargo is still open.

Freighter living is much more informal than cruise ship living. Dress is more casual, not only on deck but also in the lounge and the dining salon. Freighter days are far less organized than those on a cruise ship where social directors tend to prepare rather comprehensive menus of activities including sports competitions, dances, parties, fancy dress balls, card tournaments, movies, entertainment of all sorts, and even classes and lectures as well as guided shore excursions made easily available at each port of call. Certainly one may choose to ignore any or even all of the organized activities, but generally passengers are involved to a substantial degree. On a cargo ship the only organized activities are meals, an occasional cocktail hour, and boat and fire drills. There are no social obligations; passengers are pretty much left to their own devices. Do you want to engage in aerobic exercise? You can do it but no formal class meets each morning. Do you enjoy a casual game of cards or even serious duplicate bridge? Fine, but you will have to find like-minded collaborators among your shipmates. Reading? Sunbathing? Visits to the navigation bridge to peruse the charts, the ship's position and progress, or the collection of books and journals on seamanship, or just to talk with the mate on watch? All are easily done, but at your initiative and without the need to slide them in among organized activities you don't want to miss.

Freighter food is very good. Remember you generally eat with the ship's officers and meals of poor quality are unlikely. On some ships there is no menu choice except at breakfast; on others choices are available at each meal, but not the wide selection of gourmet dishes which often grace the dining tables of cruise ships. Many cargo ships serve a simple afternoon tea and all freighters make snacks available on a "serve yourself" basis. Some cargo ships provide a small refrigerator in each stateroom so passengers may stock their favorite beverages and foods if they wish to do so. Food service on cruise ships is not only rich, plentiful, and varied, but as a rule it is elegantly served. If you want early bird coffee and Danish, breakfast, morning bouillon, luncheon, (buffet on deck or served in the dining room), afternoon tea, dinner, and a midnight buffet all elaborately done you must sail in a cruise ship. Freighter cuisine is first class but not exotic. Dining on a freighter is more like dining as a guest in a comfortable family setting while dining on a cruise ship is more like going regularly to a posh restaurant. We hasten to amend these comments on food service by acknowledging the emergence of cafeteria style dining on some cruise ships as a means of containing costs. We leave to your contemplation the contrasts and comparisons to be made between a cafeteria format and the dining salon of a cargo ship.

Freighters are for people who are content with creating their own amusements. People who are comfortable not being sure of their exact itineraries, departure or arrival times are more likely to be happy with freighter life. People who love the sea, who enjoy reading and conversation, people who are easy going and amiable, who get along with others and are willing to adapt and accommodate are more likely to be happy on a working cargo ship. People who enjoy observing the activities of a freighter crew and the longshoremen who unload and load the cargo in port are more likely to enjoy cargo ship cruising. Finally, people who fully accept the premise that the ship and its crew exist to move goods around the world and that passengers are along for the ride rather than being the ship's primary concern are more likely to be happy on a freighter. There is time on a cargo ship: time to relax, sleep, read, converse, to feel the majesty of the ocean; to anticipate and then savor one glorious sunset after another; to view the sighting of another ship as an event; to watch for whales, dolphin, and flying fish; to wait with anticipation for the first smudge on the horizon which heralds your ship's approach to its next landfall. On the other hand there is time to spend a series of days under cloudy skies, in hazy or foggy weather without sighting another vessel. If you are wondering what you would do with all that time then be sure you develop a satisfactory answer before booking passage on a cargo ship.

Have we said enough to convince you that freighter voyaging is not for you? Well and good! It is certainly better to make that decision in your living room rather than on the deck of a cargo ship half-way across the Pacific Ocean. Are you still interested? Wonderful! Read on to learn more about life on a freighter cruise and how you can try it for yourself.

Passenger Facilities

Freighter staterooms are very large when measured by cruise ship standards. Unless you have occupied the most spacious cruise ship accommodations you will be pleasantly surprised when you walk into your first freighter stateroom. To begin with it will be larger than all but the most expensive staterooms on cruise ships. Second, there will be two twin beds or built-in bunks, not one lower and one upper. Third, there will be tables, chairs, a sofa, and enough closet and drawer space for the most extravagant packer. Fourth, the chances are you will have full size windows (not portholes) perhaps on two bulkheads since virtually all freighter staterooms are outside rooms. Fifth, you will have a private bathroom with a shower and, in some cases, a bathtub. A ship we were on recently provided us a stateroom that was 16 feet by 16 feet plus bath. Our twin beds could be arranged as conventional twins or moved together to form a king-sized bed. We had an office-sized desk with upholstered chair, a sofa and upholstered pull-up chair, a table and a refrigerator. There was plenty of closet and drawer space and a bookshelf. A radio/tape deck wired to the ship's antenna was provided as well as an excellent desk lamp. One window faced forward and one faced the starboard side. There were shades and drapes for both windows and the floor was carpeted. We were two decks below the bridge and three decks above the dining salon and lounge. For our next cargo ship voyage we are booked on a ship which provides TV/VCRs in each stateroom.

Most freighters have a comfortably furnished lounge often shared with the ship's officers. On some ships low cost beverage service is available in or near the lounge; on other ships passengers may buy alcoholic beverages by the bottle or case from the ship's slop chest (slang for ship's store) which stocks beverages, snacks, and sundries for the convenience of the crew and passengers. On a few ships alcoholic beverages may be brought on board by a passenger but are not available for sale on the ship. Fruit juices, soft drinks and mixes are routinely available. Lounges generally have a collection of paperback books augmented by each new complement of officers and passengers. There is no assurance that you will find just the books you have been pining to read in your ship's collection so it would be wise to bring those titles with you. Table games are widely available, but if you have a favorite you hope to enjoy you should bring it along also. In addition to comfortable chairs and sofas the lounge will have tables and chairs for games and letter writing and typically a radio and television receiver as well as a VCR and a tape library.

You can expect a single sitting for meals. Dinner might be served as early as 5:00 p.m. but on many ships it will be served at 6:00. Breakfast from 7:30 to 8:30 and lunch between 11:30 and 12:30 are good bets. Many ships offer tea at 3:00 p.m. and typically you will find the pantry stocked with cold cuts, cheese, jams, condiments, fruit, juices, coffee, tea, and hot chocolate for the passengers and crew. Your meals will be served by a steward and usually the same person will make your beds and clean your stateroom and bath. The amount of other service provided varies from ship to ship. Some include providing fresh ice water daily in each stateroom, for example. Some captains have the steward serve as a conduit between the passengers' needs and the ship's services such as the posting of letters, the acquisition of deck chairs, soap, detergent, irons and ironing boards, and the like. On other ships the passengers are treated more like crew members who are invited and expected to see to their own needs asking for help only when they don't know how to accomplish something on their own. Virtually all ships have an automatic washer and clothes dryer which is available to the passengers. The steward will provide clean sheets, pillow cases, and towels on a regular basis. Personal laundry is handled by the passenger. Be sure to bring some clothes pins and a light line for drying the articles you wish to wash in your bathroom rather than in the washing machine. You will need some liquid detergent and some Woolite for such hand washes. Also, you will find having a product such as Spray and Wash useful because the chances of getting some grease on your clothing are relatively good. The ship generally provides the detergent to be used in the washing machine.

General Cargo or Container Ships

Essentially there are four generic types of cargo ships: tankers, which carry liquid cargo in bulk such as crude oil or petroleum products; bulk carriers, which carry grains or dry chemicals, ores, or coal in bulk; break-bulk or general cargo ships, which carry a variety of cargo such as bagged products and food stuffs, refrigerated cargo such as fresh fruit or meat, palletized cargo of all sorts, machinery, vehicles, bulk materials, and containers each one packed by the sender and handled by both the ports and the ship as one cargo unit; and container ships, which carry only containers. Tankers never carry passengers. Bulk carriers rarely carry passengers although there are some plying the North America-Europe routes. Later in this chapter we will tell you how to find out which ships are available and how to book passage but for now let's consider features and the pro's and con's of general cargo and bulk carriers contrasted with container ships. Container ships represent the newer technology in cargo handling. A manufacturer packs a 20 foot or 40 foot long steel container at his factory. It will then be loaded on a railroad car or a special semi-trailer , delivered to a port, loaded onto a ship, off-loaded at another port, and delivered by barge, train , or truck to the receiver without handling anything except the standardized container. Large cranes designed specifically for moving containers are employed and each phase of the transport operation is accomplished with a minimum of handling. Each 40 foot container can hold up to about 30 tons of cargo so that means cargo can be loaded and unloaded at up to 30 tons per move. This is wonderful from the point of view of efficiency and it minimizes port time. Contrast cargo handling on a container ship to that on a break-bulk ship. Cargo which is not in containers is often stacked in warehouses in bags or on pallets which can be moved around the docks by fork lifts, or in bundles strapped with steel tape or in crates. Some cargo such as cars, trucks, or mobile machinery is handled without any packing or crating. Typically the ship's hoists are used to load and unload cargo from dock to ship to dock. Cargo must be loaded with care in the ship's holds and on its main deck. Most cargo is moved in increments much less than 30 tons. In short, a break-bulk ship is not nearly as efficient in cargo handling as a container ship. In most ports it is rare for a container ship to stay more than one day. On a recent voyage we made in a container ship the average port time for 16 ports was 14 hours. General cargo (break-bulk) ships sometimes stay in a port for only one day but often they are there much longer. The longest time we have been in a port on a general cargo ship was fifteen days. We have had several five to eight day stays and a large number of two to four day stays. Which is better for the passenger? Well, that depends on what the passenger likes. If what is desired is a long leisurely sea voyage where ample port time is all right, but not essential to the happiness of the voyager, then a high technology container ship will be just fine. On the other hand, if having greater time to explore port cities and their environs or for taking excursions inland is regarded as an essential aspect of one's cruise, then a container ship may not be the wise choice. Whether you think general cargo or container ships sound like your favorite is not the only issue. The fact is that before many more years roll by there will be only a few general cargo ships in intercontinental service available to book. They simply cannot compete with container technology. For now you have some choice; in the future your choices may be limited to which container ships to select. For those who yearn for copious amounts of port time all is not about to be lost. There are container ship itineraries which include ports which are often not as efficient as those in Europe, the Far East, and North America. Moreover there are itineraries which allow passengers to lay over and come home on a later ship. Having said all this, if you still prefer to sail in a general cargo ship, we encourage you to book passage sooner rather than later. One day there will be no further opportunity to do so. There are a few bulk carriers which accommodate passengers. They, like general cargo ships, require more loading and off-loading time than do container ships. Loading some bulk cargo is a messy, dirty business. The dust from cargo such as vermiculite, pottery clays, or silica can be very intrusive and even finds its way into interior deckhouse space on occasion. Once loaded and underway clean-up by hosing down the exterior of the deckhouse, hatch covers, and decks is an early order of business and, as the saying goes, there is, "No problem!"

Days at Sea

Your ship drops her harbor pilot; his launch pulls away and immediately the ship's engine takes up its steady cruising speed beat. The harbor's mouth recedes in your ship's wake, becomes indistinct and blends into the shoreline which, in turn, recedes. In due course the shoreline itself disappears below the horizon and for the next several days the sea and sky are your world. The reading, sunbathing, exercising, and conversing you do as the hours roll by are pleasant diversions but the principal reality of your days at sea (if you allow yourself the luxury) is you on a ship on an infinite sea beneath an infinite sky. Just think, no telephone calls! No appointment schedule! No time clock! No day-to-day problems like automobiles with dead batteries, freeway traffic, subway crowds! Time to think, or to avoid thinking; Time to read, to walk, to talk, to sit and watch the sea creaming along the ship's side and foaming in its wake. There is time to soak up the sun and, later in the day, to watch it set leaving remembrances of its warmth and light painted across the sky in oranges, roses, and reds before, pulling these colors behind, it returns the sky to its black velvet state filled with more stars than most city dwellers ever see. Becoming increasingly attune to the sea and the sky leads to one of the greatest bonuses of sailing in freighters: the opportunity to contemplate oneself in the infinite universe and to achieve a measure of tranquillity and inner peace.

Here are a few of the events which season the constant ship-sea-sky world. The weather: wind, sun, precipitation, haze, fog, white caps, waves, spray, foam, decks dry and decks wet, or even partially awash. Passing another ship, particularly at short range; you can heighten this experience by taking a pair of binoculars with you. Passing an ocean-going yacht (much rarer than sighting another cargo ship). Passing near islands, capes, continental shorelines, and through straits. Binoculars enhance your enjoyment in these situations also. Spotting dolphin, particularly if they decide to play with the bow of your ship by jumping across it from side to side at 18 knots! Seeing whales as they surface and blow. Marveling at the distances flying fish can glide through the air before reentering the sea. Approaching a harbor is always a special time. The anticipation of once again being ashore is part of it, but also there are the steps necessary to maneuver a large ship into a harbor and to the designated berth. It is a fascinating and compelling business, from boarding the pilot to securing the last line and moving the ship the final three meters along the dock, a business which captures the attention of every passenger. In addition to radio and radar, ships receive weather updates including map data by FAX, the ship's position from satellite-based navigation systems, and depth of water beneath the keel by echo-sounding equipment. Ships use signal flags and pay close attention to the buoys and lights that mark channels and help pinpoint the ship's location when navigating in confined waters. You can learn as much as you would like to learn about these systems from the navigation officers of your ship. In addition to what they can show and demonstrate for you on the bridge they can also provide reference material in case you want to delve more deeply. We include a few of the basics to whet your whistle. Let's begin with the wind.

The Beaufort Scale
        In order to be able to communicate information about wind and sea conditions a classification system known as the Beaufort Scale was developed by Admiral Beaufort and introduced into the British Navy early in the nineteenth century. Today it is in use throughout the world. The scale consists of 13 wind force levels. Each is defined in terms of wind velocity

in knots, a descriptive term, and a brief characterization of the sea conditions induced. Here are the Beaufort Scale categories.

Beaufort Wind Force	Mean Wind Speed in Knots	Limits of Wind Speed in Knots	Description	Sea Criterion
0	00	Less than 1	Calm	Sea like a mirror.
1	02	1-3	Light air	Ripples with appearance of scales are formed, without foam crests.
2	05	4-6	Light breeze	Small wavelets, still short but more pronounced. Crests have glassy appearance and do not break.
3	09	7-10	Gentle breeze	Large wavelets. Crests beginning to break. Foam of glassy appearance. Perhaps scattered white caps.
4	13	11-16	Moderate breeze	Small waves becoming longer. Fairly frequent white caps.
5	19	17-21	Fresh breeze	Moderate waves taking a more pronounced long form; many white caps.
6	24	22-27	Strong breeze	Large waves begin to form; white foam crests are more extensive everywhere.
7	30	28-33	Near gale	Sea heaps up; white foam from breaking waves begins to be blown in streaks.
8	37	34-40	Gale	Moderately high waves of greater length; edges of crests begin to break into spindrift. Foam is blown in well-marked streaks.
9	44	41-47	Strong gale	High waves. Dense streaks of foam. Crests of waves begin to topple, tumble, and roll over. Spray may affect visibility.

10	52	48-55	Storm	Very high waves with over-hanging crests. Great patches of foam are blown in dense white streaks. Sea surface appears white. Tumbling is heavy. Visibility is affected.
11	60	56-63	Violent Storm	Exceptionally high waves. Sea foam-covered. Wave crests blown into froth. Visibility is affected.
12	—	above 63	Hurricane force	Air filled with foam and spray. Sea completely white. Visibility is very seriously affected.

Reading Buoys

Buoys are used to define navigable channels and to mark areas which are to be avoided. The three R's of piloting ships in bays, harbors, rivers, and other confined waters are "red, right, and return." A ship which is returning to port or navigating up a river will find the red buoys on the right side of the proper channel. These red buoys are labeled with even numbers which grow larger as you come in from the sea. Numbers followed by capital letters simply indicate that buoys have been inserted in the sequence but that renumbering has not yet been done. Black buoys mark the left side of the channel as a ship enters from the sea and are labeled with odd numbers. A buoy painted with red and black horizontal bands marks an obstruction at the intersection of two channels while vertically striped buoys painted black and white indicate the center of a channel. Yellow buoys mark quarantine anchorages and white buoys mark unrestricted anchorages. White buoys with green tops indicate a dredging operation and black and white banded buoys mark the boundaries of fish trap and net areas. Reflectors are used on unlighted buoys, but channel buoys are often lighted. Those which flash at a regular frequency of not more than one flash every two seconds indicate ordinary channel markers; more rapidly flashing lights are used when special caution is required. Rapidly flashing lights with dark intervals of about four seconds are used on red and black banded buoys, White lights which emit a short flash followed by a long flash about eight times per minute are mounted on black and white vertically striped buoys.

Flying Flags

In the International Flag Code each letter and each digit is represented by its own flag. One to five flags may be hoisted to spell words or have a specified meaning in the International Flag Code. For example, hoisting the flag for the letter *D* means the ship is having trouble steering. Hoisting the flag for the letter *B* means the ship is carrying hazardous material as part of its cargo. Generally each ship flies the flag of its nation of registry as well as the flag of the host country when in port or when sailing in territorial waters. Flags for the letters of the alphabet and the digits are shown on page 78 and a list of the flags used for a selected list of messages is included below for your convenience.

Selected Messages Using the International Flag Code

Flag	Message
B	I am taking in, discharging, or carrying dangerous goods.
D	I am having difficulty steering.
G	I require a pilot.
H	I have a pilot on board.
M	My vessel is stopped and is making no way through the water.
O	Man overboard.
P	(In harbor) All aboard. Vessel is about to sail.
W	I require medical assistance.
Y	I am dragging my anchor.
Z	I require a tug.

Shore Time

One of the great pleasures of a cargo ship voyage is going ashore at the ports called on by your vessel. Sometimes the length of a freighter's stay in port is much greater than it is

International Flag Code

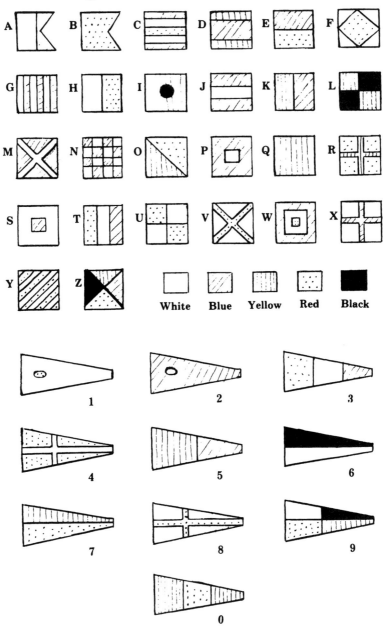

White   Blue   Yellow   Red   Black

with a cruise ship. General cargo ships which load a variety of goods packaged in a variety of ways are often in a port two to three days and, if berthing space is tight, a ship may spend additional days in the harbor's anchorage waiting for a spot at a dock. Container ships, on the other hand, spend much less time waiting for a berth and much less time at the dock unloading and loading. Their port time is rarely more than 24 hours and may be as short as eight hours.

Unlike a cruise ship a freighter docking in a cargo-handling port does not make a resounding impact on the local scene. A number of years ago when our P & O passenger ship docked at Suva, the capitol of Fiji, the police band was playing on the quay and it looked like every taxi driver on the entire island had turned out to meet the ship in order to persuade disembarking passengers that the only sensible thing to do was hire his vehicle for a morning's guided tour of the city and countryside. The entire city seemed to react to the arrival of our ship and its several hundred passengers. Even the formal guard mount and changing of the guard at Government House was coordinated with the ship's schedule. That afternoon, as the time for our ship to leave Suva approached, it was all we could do to negotiate the final two blocks from the center of town to the quay. The walks were lined with booths filled with souvenir merchandise of all kinds. The proprietors and their hawkers became more and more frenzied in their efforts to sell their wares as the passengers streamed by on their way back to the ship. Now you might thoroughly enjoy being part of such a scene or you might abhor it; that's a matter of personal preference. Perhaps some passengers' reactions were closely related to the digestibility of the curried dishes they sampled at lunch! One thing is certain however; in Suva our arrival, shore time, and departure were matters of more than passing interest to the local economy.

Arriving by cargo ship is in sharp contrast to the frenetic scenes of our day in Suva. After all, there is only a handful of people involved, not several hundred vacationing tourists.

Moreover, freighters dock in port facilities which are generally not open to unauthorized persons. Compared to a cruise ship, a cargo ship's arrival is a rather private affair which goes less noticed by the tourist and souvenir industries alike. This lack of notice puts more responsibility for planning good shore time on the cargo ship passenger and provides the chance to blend into the local scene and experience the foreign port city in ways which are largely unavailable to cruise ship passengers. Ports differ on the attention paid to berthing cargo ships. In North America, Europe, Japan, Australia, New Zealand, and many South American ports the tourist and souvenir industries pay no special heed. In many third world ports you are more likely to draw attention. In Mombassa, travel agents came on board seeking to sell safari packages. Souvenir and handicraft items were hawked on board or on the dock in many less affluent ports. In some ports the ship's agent will know how to arrange conducted tours and some passengers will welcome such activities. But there are many other options so here are a few suggestions to enhance your days (and evenings) in port.

First, if your berth is within walking distance of the city's center, walk in, find the local government tourist information office, and pick up whatever literature is available on the city and the region. Be sure to include a bus route map, a subway system map, and a city map. Talk to the people in the office to find out what they might suggest. Ask them how to get to the places you may already have identified as ones you would like to visit. Find out where the buses converge, the location of the railroad station, inter-city bus terminal, post office, bank or money exchange. Mark these points on your map. If your stay is more than a day or two you are likely to visit all these locations. Are you a beach buff? If so, ask where the best ones are and how to get to them via public transportation. Depending on what part of the world you are in you may want to inquire as to whether any of the beaches are topless or nude. It's your choice, but you are better off forewarned. City buses and subways go just about anywhere you might wish to go and they are far cheaper than taxies unless four or five are traveling together. If you have sufficient time it really doesn't matter if you happen to take a wrong bus or even get "lost" on the outskirts of a town. You can always get on another bus or subway train.

If your ship is only in port for a few hours then some of the suggestions above don't apply. Time becomes an overriding factor and a taxi to town may be well worth the added expense. Stopping at the Tourist Information Office is still a good idea but an even better idea is to have at least a partially formed plan of what you will be doing before you disembark and head for the port gate. By all means bring guide books, pamphlets, pocket atlases and phrase lists for the languages you will encounter during your voyage. You can do some advance planning and preparation as you sail toward your next port of call. The ship's officers might be helpful as well. Hopefully the ship will have a collection of brochures and maps picked up by passengers on prior voyages. These may even include notes written by former passengers telling you how to get from the port to the city's center or to other points of interest. The idea is to have a plan and some alternatives in mind because your first day ashore may also be your last day ashore.

Everything you have learned about getting along in a foreign city from other travels applies to freighter ports of call except for one thing: as a passenger on a cargo ship it need not cost very much at all. Your ship is your hotel and your restaurant for as many meals as you like. We generally skip lunch on board and eat something very light as we spend the day on shore. Often this means carrying fruit, bread, and cheese with us when we leave the ship for the day. Do you like museums, cathedrals, temples, art galleries? Do you enjoy shopping in malls, department stores, small shops, or open air market stalls? If you are on a general cargo ship you may have time for them all; on a container ship you probably must make some choices. Would a bus or train ride of two or three hours bring you to an attraction you would really like to reach? If there is time do it! While in the Italian port city of Livorno we spent one day on the Italian Riviera at Portofino, a three hour train ride up the Italian coast. Another day found us in Florence, one and one-half hours from Livorno by train. It was easy to do. Bus and train schedules are posted in terminals and with a little practice they are easy to read. As related in chapter one we left our ship berthed at Port Said, Egypt and spent three days in Cairo and Luxor visiting museums, the Pyramids, and the Valley of the Kings. You can do the same thing. Be aware that most ticket agents are not English-speaking, but information booths are often staffed by multi-lingual attendants and notes and impromptu sign language help bridge the communication gap. Finally, the secret is to relax and relish the strangeness. After all, one reason for seeing the world is to experience something different, isn't it? Moving around port cities and the surrounding countryside like the local population does it is part of the fun and exhilaration of cargo ship cruising. If time permits we recommend eschewing taxies, guided tours populated by American tourists, and "name brand" hotels in order to taste the rest of the world. Remember, you have the reassurance of the ship. Its air-conditioned dining salon, decks, lounge, and your familiar stateroom are ever-present havens in which to relax after a long day ashore.

What Does It Cost?

We have mentioned ways of minimizing expenses while spending time ashore as your ship unloads and loads cargo, but we haven't discussed the cost of purchasing space on cargo ships. Later in this chapter you will find listings of passenger-carrying freighter and cargo liner routes. One of the things you will learn by reading these listings is that cargo ship cruising is a relatively inexpensive way to travel. The daily costs are about one-half to two-thirds as much as lower end cruise ship rates and represent excellent value for your travel dollar. Just a few years ago we made a 77 day voyage with Yugolinia, a Yugoslav shipping company. Due to the happy coincidence of a very favorable exchange rate between U.S. dollars and Yugoslavian dinars plus the extension of the voyage well beyond its projected 50 days the cost was a bit less than $25 per day per person! Even though this was a recent occurrence we do not expect to enjoy such an inexpensive voyage again. Just think: 77 days lodging, three meals per day, plus an 18,000 mile cruise for $1900 per person. More recently we made an 84 day voyage with Projex Line, a German shipping company, for $94 per day per person. There are freighter cruises available at the $75 per day level at this time, but most are closer to $100 per day. As with most markets it pays to watch for discounts! We are scheduled to sail to Australia and New Zealand from the east coast of the United States. The low season fare diminished by a further discount plus a small rebate from the agent we are using resulted in a $61 per day cost for the projected 70 day round trip.

Are you still interested? Would you like to learn what itineraries are currently available, their present cost, and how to go about booking passage? The rest of this chapter is devoted to these questions.

Where Can I Go?

As you read the listings of passenger carrying freighters in this section you will see that it is possible to cruise to a great many ports throughout the world on cargo ships. We have listed the cargo ship services which embark passengers in the United States and Canada and have also included cargo ship services which embark passengers elsewhere in the world if we know of a travel agent or ship's agent in North America who handles passenger bookings for the service. By studying these listings you will gain a good picture of the routes currently available. Should you become seriously interested in booking a freighter cruise whose port of embarkation is outside North America be sure to gain a clear understanding of the predictability of the ship's schedule. Projected embarkation dates for general cargo ships ordinarily are quite tentative until a very short time before departure. Projected dates for container ships are also tentative but these vessels tend to adhere much more closely to projected schedules. It is important for you to plan your travel to the port of embarkation so that you arrive in time but you will probably also be interested in minimizing the cost of waiting for your ship and of the airfare to the embarkation city. Doing this is easiest if the port of embarkation is in North America, harder (but manageable) if the port of embarkation is overseas and you are in close consultative contact with an agent, and hardest of all if you are embarking overseas and have no easy consultative contact with an agent.

The listings contain information which is as current as publishing deadlines allow and the accuracy of the entries is controlled by every means available. Nevertheless fares, itineraries, schedules, age limits, and other data are all subject to change without notice and should be confirmed. We cannot assume responsibility for errors, omissions, or revisions which will inevitably occur over time. An excellent source for reasonably up-to-date listings of passenger-carrying freighters is *The Official Steamship Guide International* which is published quarterly by Transportation Guides, Inc., 9111 Cross Park Drive, Suite D-247, Knoxville, TN 37923. A domestic subscription is $83.00 per year (in Canada, $88.00). Some travel agents and libraries subscribe to this publication so there is no compelling reason for having your own subscription. The passenger freighter entries and associated advertisements typically are limited to five or six pages of a much longer publication. If you would like to receive information and listings regularly in the mail you should consider subscribing to the newsletters published by Freighter World Cruises, Inc., 180 South Lake Ave., Suite 335, Pasadena, CA 91101; telephone 818-449-6830 and/or TravLtips Cruise and Freighter Travel Association, 163-07 Depot Road, P.O. Box 580218, Flushing, NY 11358-0218; telephone 800-872-8584. Both of these organizations specialize in freighter travel and broker space on most of the routings that would be of interest.

The passenger carrying freighter routes listed below are organized by the geographic area the ship serves. These include Europe and the Mediterranean Basin; Africa and the Indian Ocean; South America and the Caribbean; and Around the World. For each route we give the name of the shipping company, the itinerary, the projected length of the cruise, the maximum number of passengers, the age limit, the current cost of a round trip cruise, and the type of cargo ship (container, bulk carrier, break-bulk, or combination) to the extent these data are available. For those routes on which many one-way sailings are booked the one-way fares are included. Most shipping companies will sell space for one-way passage or other segments but often wait until one or two months before embarkation to offer such space since they prefer to book round trip passengers. If a shipping company is served by an exclusive passenger agent that agent is referenced for your convenience. For all other listings we recommend contacting Freighter World Cruises, TravLtips (both referenced above), or Freighter Cruise Service, 5925 Monkland Ave., Suite 103, Montreal, Que., Canada H4A1G71 telephone 514-481-0447. These freighter specialists will be able to provide additional details about specific ships, choice of accommodations, on-board amenities, projected sailing dates, and up to the minute fares. They will be happy to wait-list you and secure bookings for you. Their fee will be paid by the shipping company and will not affect the price to you.

Be sure to find out about port taxes and custom or immigration fees which may be charged in addition to the fare quoted. In addition your agent will let you know about medical examinations and immunizations which may be required, visas needed if any, and trip interruption, emergency medical, and medical evacuation insurance available for you. We will have more to say on these topics in the next chapter.

Passenger-Carrying Freighter Routes

Europe and the Mediterranean
Atlantic Conbulk Services. From Montreal to Antwerp, Rotterdam or Dunkirk, Montreal. 30-35 days. 6 passengers. Age limit: 82. $2875 single or double; one-way eastbound $1525; westbound $1350. Container/bulk service.

Containerships Reederei. From Los Angeles transit Panama Canal, Puerto Cabello, Venez., Valencia, Sp., Livorno and Valdo Ligure, It., La Guaira, Venez., transit Panama Canal, Los Angeles, Vancouver, Portland, Oakland, Los Angeles. About 48 days L.A. to L.A.; about 59 days Vancouver to Vancouver. 6 passengers. Age limit: 79. L.A. to L.A. $5000-$5500 pp double, $5500 single. Vancouver to Vancouver $5900-$6490 double, $6490 single. Container service.

Grimaldi Freighter Cruises. From Antwerp, Southampton, or Goteburg, Swed., to Piraeus, Gr., Limmasol, Cyp., Ashdad, Isr., an Italian port. 12 passengers. No age limit. $2620 pp double, $3920 single; sofa berth for child with 2 ticketed adults $1760.

Mineral Shipping (PTE.) Ltd. From Savannah usually to several ports in Italy and Greece, sometimes to Brazil returning to east coast of USA. About 70 days. 12 passengers. Age limit:82. $5775 pp double, $6300 single. If voyage is less than 70 days refund of $82.50/day double, $90/day single. If more than 70 days, the same per diem is added. Bulk service.

Mineral Shipping (PTE.) Ltd. From Savannah usually to 2 ports in the Netherlands, return to east coast of USA. About 32-35 days. $2750 single or double, $1400 one way. Bulk Service.

Polish Ocean Lines. Agent: Gdynia America Line, Inc., P.O. Box 10510, New Brunswick, NJ 08905-0510. 908-412-6000 Ext. 107, Fax: 908-757-9545. From Gdynia to Western European ports; ports in Morroco, Libya, Tunisia, Egypt, Israel, Turkey, Syria, Cyprus; Gdynia. Length of voyage varies, but is shorter on container ships than on general cargo ships. Age limit: 75. $800-$1000 pp double, add 16% for single.

United Baltic Corp. From Felixstowe and Hull to Turku, Helsinki, Hamina, and Rauma, Finland and return

From Hull to Gdynia, Poland and return.
Durations, fares, and age limitations available from United Baltic Corp., Dexter House, 2 Royal Mint Court, London EC3N 4XX UK. Tel. 071-265-0808.

Australia, New Zealand, Far East, Pacific

Blue Star. From Jacksonville, transit Panama Canal to Auckland, Melbourne, Sydney, Brisbane, Port Chalmers, Wellington, Auckland, Philadelphia. About 70 days. 10 passengers. Age limit: 79. High season: $6800-$7700 pp double, $7600-$8500 single. Low season: $5400-$6150 pp double,$6100-$6800 single. One-way and sea/air fares available. Container service.

Blue Star. From Seattle to Oakland, Los Angeles, Suva (Fiji).Auckland, Sydney, Melbourne, Wellington, Auckland, Suva, Seattle. About 42-45 days. 12 passengers. Age limit: 79. From $3975 pp double, $4775 single. One-way and sea/air fares available. Container service.

Columbus Line. From Jacksonville to New Orleans, Houston, transit Panama Canal, Melbourne, Sydney, Brisbane, Auckland, Wellington, Port Chalmers, transit Panama Canal, occasionally Kingston (Jamaica), Philadelphia. About 67 days. 8-12 passengers. Age limit: 79. High season: $6930 pp double, $8250 single. Low season: from $4620 pp double, $5280 single. One-way and sea/air fares available. Container service.

Columbus Line. From Long Beach to Auckland, Sydney, Melbourne, Brisbane, Wellington, Auckland, occasionally Suva or Honolulu, Seattle. About 46 days. 8-12 passengers. Age limit: 79. High season: $4830 pp double, $5750 single. Low season: $4370 pp double, $5290 single. Container service.

Compagnie Polynesienne de Transport Maritime. From Papeete, Tahiti to Tuamotu and Marquesas Islands and return. 15 days. 77 cabin passengers plus sheltered deck space. No age limit. $2860-$3920 pp double. 50% surcharge for singles. Break-bulk service.

Egon Oldendorff Line. From Auckland to Napier, Lyttleton, Port Chalmers, Tauranga, Surabaya and Jakarta (Indonesia), Port Kelang (Malaysia), Singapore, Bangkok, Singapore, Noumea (New Caledonia), Suva (Fiji), Auckland. About 61 days. 8 passengers. Age limit: 79. $5000-$5710 double or single. One-way and sea/air fares available. Container with some break-bulk service.

Egon Oldendorff Line. From Auckland to Napier, Nelson, Timaru, Tauranga, Manila, Hong Kong, Kaoshiung or Taichung, and Keelung (Taiwan), Suva (Fiji) or Noumea (New Caledonia), Auckland. About 48 days. 8 passengers. Age limit: 79. $3935 double or single. Container with some break-bulk service.

Egon Oldendorff Line. From Auckland to Napier, Nelson, Timaru, Tauranga, Busan (S. Korea), Kitakyushu, Nakanoseki, Hiroshima, Osaka, Nagoya and Yokohama (Japan), Auckland. About 48 days. 8 passengers. Age limit: 79. $3935 double or single. Container with some break-bulk service.

Niederielbe Schiffahrtsgesellschaft Buxtehude (NSB). From Seattle to Portland, Seattle, Busan (S. Korea), Hong Kong, Kaoshiung (Taiwan), Busan, Seattle. About 35 days. 12 passengers. Age limit: 79. $2950-$3315 pp double, $3685-$3870 single. Container service.

Deutsche Seereederi Rostock. From New York to Norfolk, Savannah, Valencia (Sp.), La Spezia (It.), transit Suez Canal, Khor Fakkan (UAE), Singapore, Busan (S. Korea), Kaohsiung (Taiwan), Hong Kong, Singapore, transit Suez Canal, Larnaca (Cyp.), La Spezia, Fos sur Mer (Fr.), Valencia, New York. About 91 days. 5-8 passengers. Age limit: 79. From $9555 pp double, $10,647 single. Segments available. Container service.

Africa and Indian Ocean

Bank Line. From Savannah to Philadelphia, Baltimore, Cape Town, Port Elizabeth and Durban (S. Africa), Recife (Brazil), San Juan (PR), Vera Cruz (Mex.), Houston, New Orleans, Savannah. Usually one or more West African and South American ports are included. About 75 days. 8 passengers. Age limit: 82. $8450 pp in suite or single, $7700 pp double. Container with some break-bulk service.

Bank Line. From Durban (S. Africa) to Dar Es Salaam (Tanzania), Mombassa (Kenya), Dubai (UAE), Karachi (Pak.), Bombay, Mombassa, Durban. About 56 days. 9 passengers. Age limit: 82. $5600 double or single, $6160 for owner's suite. Break-bulk service.

Curnow Shipping. From Cardiff (UK) to Tenerife (Canary Is.), Ascension and St. Helena, Cape town. 26 days one-way. 128 passengers. No age limit. Passengers disembark at St. Helena for 6-7 days while ship calls to Ascension. $3030 pp double, $4200 single. Triples and quads. are available. Sea/air plus UK, St. Helena, and Cape Town land packages available. Combination break-bulk/passenger liner.

Grimaldi Freighter Cruises. From Tilbury (UK) to Hamburg, Rotterdam, Antwerp, various ports in West Africa and Brazil, Le Havre, Tilbury. About 55 days. 12 passengers. No age limit. $3690-$6690 pp double, $4123-$5890 single, $2990 pp in 4 berth cabin.

Polish Ocean Lines. Agent: See listing on page 87. From Szezecin to Western European port, Los Palmas (Canary Is.), Dakar, Freetown (Sierra Leone), Monrovia, Abidjan (Ivory Coast), Lagos, other African and European ports, Szcaecin. About 70-90 days. Age limit: 75. Fares on request from agent.

South America and the Caribbean
Chilean Line. From Miami to Santos, Buenos Aires, Rio Grande, Itajai, Santos, Rio de Janeiro, Vitoria (occasionally), New York, Baltimore, Charleston, Miami. About 46 days. 12 passengers. Age limit: 82. $4600 pp double, $5060 single. Container service.

Doehle Line. From Miami to Kingston (Jamaica), Rio de Janeiro, Santos, Buenos Aires, Montevideo, Rio Grande, Itajai, Santos, Vitoria, Ilheus, Kingston, New York. About 45 days. 8 passengers. Age limit: 79. $3790 pp double or single. Container service.

Egon Oldendorff. From New Orleans to Houston, Altamira (Mex.), Cartagena and Barranquilla (Col.), transit Panama Canal, Buenaventura (Col.), Guayaquil (Ecua.), Callao (Peru), San Antonio (Chile), Guayaquil, Buenaventura, transit Panama Canal, Cartagena, New Orleans. About 46 days. 10 passengers. $4300-$4850 pp double, $4850 single. Container/break-bulk service.

Ivaran Lines. From Port Elizabeth to Baltimore, Norfolk, Savannah, Miami, Rio de Janeiro, Santos, Buenos Aires, Montevideo, Rio Grande, Itajai, Santos, Rio de Janeiro, Salvador, Fortaleza, Port Elizabeth. About 44 days. 12 passengers. Age limit: 79. $6690 double or single. Container service.

Invaran Lines. From New Orleans to Houston, Rio de Janeiro, Santos, Buenos Aires, Rio Grande, Itajai or Paranagua, Santos, Rio de Janeiro or Vitoria, Salvador, Fortaleza, Bridgetown (Barbados), San Juan (PR), Vera Cruz and Altamira (Mex.), New Orleans. About 46-48 days. 88 passengers. No age limit.

Dec.-Feb: $11,760-$14,400 pp double, $9600-$11,760 single; Mar.-Oct.: $10320-$12480 pp double, $9640-$10,320 single. Sea/air fares available. Segments available. Container/break-bulk/ passenger liner service.

MC Shipping. From New York to Savannah or Jacksonville, Miami, Rio de Janeiro, Santos, Buenos Aires, Montevideo, Rio Grande, Itajai, Santos, Rio de Janeiro, Fortaleza, Norfolk, Baltimore, Philadelphia, New York. 45-50 days. Age limit: 79. $4850 pp double, $4510 single. Container service.

Polish Ocean Lines. Agent: See listing on page 87. From Gdynia to Hamburg, Antwerp or Rotterdam, Panama, Guayaquil, Callao, Valparaiso, Arica, Panama, Western European ports, Gydnia. About 80 days. Age limit: 75. $3300 pp double, add 10% for single.

Polish Ocean Lines. Agent: See listing on page 87. From Gdynia to Hamburg or Rotterdam or Antwerp, Buenos Aires, Montevideo, Santos, Paranagua, or Salvador, usually other Brazilian ports, Western European ports, Gydnia. About 90 days. Age limit: 75. About $2400 pp double, add 10% for single.

Transeste Shipping. From Long Beach to Manzanillo (Mex.), Puerto Quetzal (Guat.), Coco Solo (Pan.), transit Panama Canal, Cartagena (Col.), Rio Heina (Dom. Rep.), second call to all above ports, plus Puerto Caldera (Costa R.), Long Beach. About 28 days. 8 passengers. Age limit: 79. $2620 pp double, $2950 single.

Uniline Naviera Universal. Routings circumnavigate South America in both directions. Passengers may embark and disembark at a number of ports. Complete circumnavigation about 60 days. Segments available. 6-12 passengers. No age limit. Ports may include Paranagua, Rio de Janeiro and Santos (Brazil); Montevideo; Campana, San Nicolas, Buenos Aires, and Puerto Madryn (Argen.); Talcahuano and Valparaiso (Chile); Matarani, Callao, and Paita (Peru); Puerto Bolivar,

Guayaquil, and Esmiraldas (Ecua.); Buenaventura (Col.); Cristobal (Pan.); Cartagena (Col.); Puerto Cabello, La Guaira, and Guanta (Venez.). Full circumnavigation: $100/day, 30 days or more: $110/day, less than 30 days: $125/day. Break-bulk service.

Windjammer Barefoot Cruises. From Freeport (Bahamas) to British Virgin Islands, Leeward Islands, and other islands en route to Trinidad, and return. 26 days; one-way 13 days. 100 passengers. No age limit. Round trip $2250-$2700, one-way $1125-$1350. Deduct $100 for departures June-October. Passenger/provisioning of Windjammer sailing ships service.

Around the World

Bank Line. From Hull (UK) to Antwerp, Hamburg, Dunkirk and Le Havre (Fr.), transit Panama Canal, Papeete (Tahiti), Noumea (N. Cal.), Suva and Lantoka (Fiji), occasionally Port Vila, Vanuatu, or Honiara (Sol. Is.), Lae, Rabaul, Kimbe, and Madang (Papua New Guinea), occasionally Darwin, Singapore, transit Suez Canal, Antwerp. 110-115 days. 12 passengers. Age limit: 82. $12,125 double or single. Segments sometimes available. Break-bulk service.

Niederelbe Schiffahrtsgessellschaft Buxtehude (NSB). From Charleston, transit Panama Canal, Papeete, Noumea, Auckland, Melbourne, Sydney, Keelung (Taiwan), Hong Kong, Singapore, transit Suez Canal, Port Said (Egypt), Savona, Salerno, Felixstowe, Hamburg, Rotterdam, Dunkirk, New York. About 96 days. 10 passengers. Age limit: 79. $8640-$10,848 pp double, $11,232-$13,248 single. Container service.

NSB. From Long Beach to Oakland, Busan (S. Korea), Kaohsiung (Taiwan), Hong Kong, Singapore, Columbo (Sri Lanka), transit Suez Canal, Rotterdam, Bremmerhaven, Felixstowe, Antwerp, Le Havre, New York, Norfolk, Savannah, transit Panama Canal, Long Beach. About 77 days. 8 passengers. Age limit: 79. $9009 pp double or single. Container service.

4

GETTING READY

S ome people spend virtually no time on long-range advance planning for a cargo ship cruise. "You know," they say, "Until we have a firm offer of space which we have accepted, we really don't know whether or not we are actually going. We don't want to be disappointed and so we would rather not get excited until we're sure of going." If these words express your sentiments then just use this chapter as a check list to help you remember all the things to accomplish before you leave. But we encourage you to consider another point of view. You can think of each voyage as consisting of three parts: planning and anticipation, the voyage itself, then reminiscing and relating your experiences to family and friends. To cut short the first phase is to deprive yourself of an important and satisfying aspect of the total experience. Some people derive almost as much pleasure from anticipating and preparing for a freighter cruise as they do from the voyage itself. For them the weeks and months before embarkation can be great fun as they read about the parts of the world they hope to visit and compile the materials and equipment they want to take with them. We recommend opting for whole-hearted, enthusiastic preparation for your cruise over an extended period. Try it; you may like it!

Do Your Reading

As soon as your request for space has been acknowledged it is time to begin a program of reading about the regions of the world along your projected route. If you will be sailing in a general cargo ship it may be too early to know which ports of call you will visit. If you will be in a container ship the ports of call may be reasonably well defined at this point. In any case there is much to learn about the regions involved. What interests you most? Some people love to read accounts of the early exploratory voyages to the continents they hope to visit. An appreciation of what it was like to sail a small ship over unknown seas to unfamiliar lands provides a romantic and contemplative backdrop for a modern day voyage. The seas appear changeless over time. And even though a modern cargo ship is a far cry from a seventeenth century vessel, there are important commonalties with those who sailed those waters in an earlier age. The sky, the stars, the swell, the vastness of the ocean, the sense of man's place, albeit insignificant, in the universe as you contemplate the heavens on a clear night at sea, all are experiences to be shared with those who went before us.

Combing through a good guidebook on the continents and countries along your expected route provides an excellent introduction to the lands and peoples you may be visiting. At this point we prefer focusing on the chapters which outline the history, geography, weather, and social customs of the regions. The information on how to get around in specific cities and between port cities and other locations is important, but we like to first gain the background necessary to understand better what it is we will be experiencing. The specifics of sights to see and things to do can be attended to later and with a more informed outlook on which to base choices. Reading a good travel guide may inspire you to undertake more detailed readings in other sources. In most libraries you will find travel books covering a variety of countries, accounts of experiences living in specific countries, relevant history books, popularized anthropology books, novels whose settings are countries of interest, and magazines such as *National Geographic*. If your library has the *New York Times* or similar major newspapers in micro-storage you can run through their indices looking for articles which appear to be germane. Don't overlook the freighter newsletters you may have such as *TravLtips* or *Freighter Travel News*. These last sources provide only cursory information about people and places, but they generally have useful information about how to get around in ports of call and their environs which could prove valuable to you, We have found that reading about the people and places, both in historical and contemporary terms, is a grand way to savor the anticipatory pleasures of a contemplated cargo ship cruise. Furthermore, it enhances the time ashore during the trip because of the historical, geographic, and social awareness gained.

Not surprisingly, there is a reference book that can be a significant resource for you as you seek out good books to read. Hopefully your library has a copy or can obtain one through inter-library loan. It is M. Simony, Editor, *The Traveler's Reading Guide*, 1987, Freelance Publications. To give you an idea of what this book contains we looked up "Africa" as an example. Listed were Guidebooks, Background Reading Sources, sources on Culture and Commentary, Explorers and Explorations, Animals in Africa, History, Novels, and Travel Articles. All of these references were followed by references for areas such as Central Africa and then country-specific listings.

What About Shopping?

Another activity which some travelers like to prepare for in advance is shopping. If uncovering more favorable prices is important to you then you should window shop at home before buying overseas. In this way you can get an idea of what is being imported for sale in North America from the countries you expect to visit and you will develop a sense of what is and is not a bargain when you see it in a shop or market stall abroad. Don't forget to factor in the duty you may be paying upon your return home when making comparisons. For many finding appropriate mementos of the voyage and the ports of call is more important than being certain they have minimized the prices paid. We have come to believe that finding one or two truly nice items makes a more lasting remembrance than acquiring less desirable items from every port of call. For us touristy items just don't seem to stand the test of time.

What About Special Insurance?

The basic purpose of any insurance coverage is to protect the insured against losses which, if uninsured, the person would have to bear. If you feel that a cargo ship cruise in no way increases your risk of loss to an unacceptable level, then you have no perceived need for any special coverage. We have always felt that the longer voyages which result in putting oneself at greater distance from home and, at times, at significant distance from state of the art health care increase the risk of loss sufficiently to warrant special insurance coverage.

Your insurance agent and your travel agent should be in a position to provide both information and advice to you as you consider whether or not you should add any special coverage to the array of policies already in force on your behalf. When we have felt the need for special coverage we have purchased travel insurance from a carrier recommended by one of the travel agencies specializing in freighter cruises. Here is what was covered in a policy we purchased for a recent voyage: emergency assistance hot line via telephone or telex; health care provider referral service; medical consultation and monitoring world-wide; medical transportation for patient and attendant to nearest medical facility or back home; transportation home for accompanying dependents under age 23 after patient is in hospital for seven days; and transportation to the patient's bedside for a person selected by the patient; assistance in replacing passports, visas, vehicle registrations, and other documents lost while traveling; assistance in obtaining a legal advisor; assistance in obtaining an emergency cash transfer; trip cancellation and interruption insurance; up to $100 per day travel delay insurance; baggage insurance against loss, damage, or theft; baggage delay insurance; emergency medical and dental expense insurance. The schedule of coverage we purchased was as listed below:

Trip cancellation/interruption	$1000 pp
Travel delay	200 pp
Baggage	500 pp
Baggage delay	200 pp
Emergency medical/dental expense	3000 pp
Outpatient deductible	50 pp
Medical transportation	10,000 pp

You can expect to pay between $75 and $150 for a similar array of coverage depending on the number of days duration of your trip.

Health Care

By all means have a medical check-up before leaving. Some shipping lines request a physician's report for all prospective passengers; some lines limit this requirement to passengers beyond some specified age. While with your doctor be sure to arrange for sufficient prescription orders for any medications you are taking. Do not plan on replenishing your medicines abroad; take enough with you for the entire voyage. Keep all medicines in their original containers correctly labeled in order to avoid difficulties with customs inspections throughout your trip. As a safeguard have your doctor list the brand names and generic names of all your prescription drugs and the dosages he is prescribing on his letterhead so that you can show this list to any doctor who may treat you while you are on your cruise.

What do you do if you need a doctor's attention while away? If you are at sea and no doctor is on board, the ship's officers will treat you as best they can. At least one of them will be well trained in first aid and emergency medical procedures. They will also seek consultative assistance through the ship's communication center. In the event of a serious medical problem requiring expert medical treatment as soon as possible the ship will head for the nearest medical help available. When in port, the ship's agent is generally a reliable source of advice. If you are covered by a travel insurance policy like the one described above you should contact its advisory service for referral. In an emergency head for the most accessible big hospital. If other sources of information are not working out, a call to a United States or Canadian Embassy or Consulate should produce the names of English-speaking doctors in the area. To further prepare for the eventuality of needing a physician while abroad you can join the International Association for Medical Assistance to Travelers (IAMAT), 417 Center Street, Lewiston, New York 14092; telephone 716-754-4883. IAMAT's Canadian address is 1287 St. Clair Avenue, Toronto, Ontario M6E 1B8; telephone 416-652-0137. Membership is free. IAMAT publishes a worldwide directory of English-speaking physicians meeting IAMAT standards.

All necessary dental work should be completed before you embark on an extended cruise. A two week Pacific crossing can certainly be marred by a chronic toothache. Be sure your check-up includes a complete set of dental x-rays so that emerging problems can be spotted and treated before you leave. Having dental work done in a foreign port may prove to be either very expensive or less than satisfactory or both.

If you wear glasses or contact lenses carry an extra pair and keep a copy of your lens prescription with you so that you can replace broken or lost equipment if you must without having your eyes reexamined. Your optician should be able to sell you a small repair kit which includes a tiny screw driver and spare fasteners to tighten or reattach frames to ear pieces. Don't forget sunglasses and a high-numbered sun block; they are musts for sunny days on deck.

Immunizations

You can expect the shipping company to let you know if you must have protective immunizations for the countries you will be visiting. They will let you know what the requirements are so do not treat their report as advisory; the immunizations they list are mandatory. Your doctor, IAMAT, the United States Public Health Service, your county health officer, or your travel agent all have references which indicate both the required and the recommended immunizations for travel in various parts of the world. You may wish to have a wider range of protection than that provided by the required list alone. For example, for a recent voyage yellow fever and cholera immunizations were required. In addition we updated our polio, gamma globulin, influenza, and tetanus immunizations. Be sure to schedule your immunizations well in advance of your departure date. Some require more than one injection. Yellow fever immunization requires custom preparation of the serum and is done only by appointment at specified medical centers with at least one in each state or province. Finally, if you schedule your immunizations over time you will minimize the possibility of having any adverse reaction to the sera being administered. Your immunizations will be recorded on an International Record of Vaccinations which you should carry with you whenever you travel outside the United States or Canada.

Passports and Visas

With the exception of traveling to some western hemisphere countries, you must have a passport upon leaving the United States to enter another country, and to return. If you do not have a currently valid passport do not wait until the last moment to apply for one. Give yourself three or four months prior to your projected departure date. If you have never had a United States passport you must submit a completed Form DSP-11, Application for Passport, in person. Your application must be accompanied by (1) proof of U.S. citizenship, (2) proof of identity, (3) two photographs, and (4) fees as outlined below personally delivered to one of the following acceptance agents: a clerk of any federal or state court of record or a judge or clerk of any probate court accepting applications; a designated postal employee at selected post offices; or an agent at a Passport Agency in Boston, Chicago, Honolulu, Houston, Los Angeles, Miami, New Orleans, New York, Philadelphia, San Francisco, Seattle, Stamford, or Washington, DC; or if abroad, a U.S. consular official. If you have had a previous passport you can submit a completed Form DSP-82, Application for Passport by Mail, if (1) you can submit your most recent passport, (2) you were at least 18 years old when your most recent passport was issued, (3) your most recent passport was issued less than twelve years ago, and (4) you use the same name as on your most recent passport or you have had your name changed by marriage or court order and can submit proper documentation to reflect your name changes. The allowable ways in which you may prove your identity are specified. Your photographs must be identical photographs of you alone, sufficiently recent to be a good likeness (normally taken within the past six months) two by two inches in size, with the image size from bottom of chin to top of head (including hair) of between one and one and three-eighths inches. Photographs must be clean, front view, full face, taken in normal street attire, without a hat or dark glasses, and printed on thin paper with a plain light (white or off-white) background. They may be black and white or color. They must be capable of withstanding a mounting temperature of 225° Fahrenheit (107° Celsius). Photographs retouched so that your appearance is changed are unacceptable. Snapshots, most vending machine prints, and magazine or full-length photographs are unacceptable. If you are 18 years of age or older submit a fee of $65. Your passport will be valid for ten years from the date of issue except where limited by the Secretary of State to a shorter period. For applicants under 18 years of age submit a fee of $40. Pay fees by check or money order. If abroad you may pay the foreign currency equivalent or use a check drawn on a U.S. bank. Be sure to read carefully the complete directions which are printed on DSP-11 or DSP-82 to insure that you submit a valid passport application.

Some countries require visas before allowing entry to holders of valid passports. U.S. Passport Agencies do not issue visas; it is your responsibility to obtain them from the embassy or consular offices of the country to be visited. Your travel agent will have a list of entry requirements for each country as well as the addresses to which visa applications are to be sent in the United States. In some cases visas may be obtained at the port of entry; in most cases you are expected to have your visa before leaving the United States. One reason for obtaining your passport well in advance of your departure is to allow enough time for visa acquisition. Visas are entered in your passport by the embassy or consular personnel of the country to be visited. This means that your passport together with a completed visa application (and in some cases, photographs) must be submitted in order to get a visa. If you need several, the time for sending and receiving the necessary documents mounts up rapidly. One way to shorten this time is to hand-deliver your passport and visa applications and personally pick up your passport and visa country by country. This works reasonably well if you live near Washington, New York, or Chicago and have the time to devote to this activity. Otherwise it is just about impossible. An alternative way to shorten the time required is to have your travel agent supply you with the visa application forms you need, obtain any photographs required, and then contact an agent in Washington or New York who specializes in visa acquisitions. The agent will deliver and pick up your documents at the appropriate embassies or consulates. After obtaining all necessary visas, your passport with visas imprinted will be returned to you. There is a fairly steep fee for such custom service, but if time is a problem you'll have little choice. Your travel agent can suggest agents who will perform this service for you. In the past we have used Travisa, 2122 P Street, NW, Washington DC 20037; telephone 800-222-2589 or 202-463-6166. Once again, get your passport early to avoid the anxiety of waiting for the return of your passport with your visas entered as your embarkation date approaches.

Clothing, Luggage, and Equipment

Dress on a working cargo ship is informal. Men will not need suits, blazers, or ties; women will not need dressy suits, dresses, and the like aboard ship. Sports clothes, shirts and slacks, jeans, shorts, swimming trunks, a sweater and jacket, plus a cap or hat of some sort are the essentials for a man on board a cargo ship. Ladies need slacks, skirts, shorts, sport tops, blouses, a sweater and jacket or raincoat, and a swimsuit. Remember that grease spots are easy to pick up on a freighter so you should bring clothing that does not require dry cleaning. You should also bring clothing that requires little or no ironing unless you enjoy that sort of activity. Be sure to have comfortable, broken-in, walking shoes. Bring tennis shoes or other light weight footwear with composition or rubber soles and heels for the safe negotiation of decks and ship's ladders (stairs). To these essentials add one or two semi-dressy outfits for ship's parties or for dinner or an evening ashore if you wish to do so. We have found that dressy clothing is not needed at all but we recognize that people differ on what they wish to wear. If your voyage takes you to the Southern Hemisphere remember that the seasons are reversed. Remember, too, that temperatures at sea are generally cooler than temperatures ashore. Check temperature averages for the months you will be away in the places you will visit and select appropriate clothing. Remember at sea there is always a breeze on deck caused by the velocity of the ship even if the air is dead calm.

The amount and variety of equipment you include is clearly a matter of personal choice. Most people bring a camera;

some bring extensive photographic equipment. A battery pack video camera is more and more commonplace, particularly as this equipment has become available in smaller, lighter forms. In any case be sure to bring enough film or tape for the entire voyage. By doing so you will avoid seeking just the stock you want in port cities. Equally important: film prices tend to be markedly higher overseas than they are in North America. Generally we plan on having our film processed after returning home; the costs tend to be lower and the risk of losing film is reduced. There are, however, an increasing number of one hour film processing outlets throughout the world so you can consider having developing and printing done as your voyage progresses. In case you fly to your port of embarkation or fly home after your cruise be sure to remove film from your luggage when arriving at the airport so that it does not pass through an x-ray screening device. X-rays can ruin film and repeated exposures to even very low level radiation can be enough to spoil your efforts to create a pictorial history of your voyage.

Many cargo ship travelers enjoy using binoculars on shipboard. Most ships pass at a distance which demands optical magnification if any detail is to be seen. The same is true of islands being passed and shores being approached. Binoculars are not essential, but they add to the enjoyment of encounters at sea. With some exceptions, cargo ship staterooms are not equipped with radio-cassette players. Find out about your ship and, if such equipment is not provided, consider bringing a radio that has FM, SW, and MW bands. Usually there are antenna jacks in the staterooms but you should check this detail also. On foreign flag vessels the electrical service will almost certainly not be 110 volt/ 60 amperes and you will need both a transformer and appropriate receptacle plug. The same goes for any other electrical appliance you hope to use on board. By all means bring brochures, pamphlets, maps, and guide books for the regions being visited. A map large enough in scope to encompass the entire itinerary on which the ship's progress can be charted is nice to have and it will remain a treasured

keepsake of the cruise. Don't forget writing paper, a notebook, envelopes, scotch tape, magazines, and books. Also include sun block, playing cards, table games, and favorite movies on video tape. If your ports of call include some in less developed areas you may want to bring a supply of gifts to hand out. Small bars of soap have been greatly appreciated by women we have encountered. Ball point pens seem to please, particularly if they are labeled from your locale or nation.

The luggage you carry is not as crucial a matter for cargo ship travel as it sometimes is for other sorts of trips. Remember, one of the finest advantages of freighter life is that after unpacking your suitcases upon coming on board you don't have to use them again until the end of the voyage. There is no packing and unpacking throughout your trip unless you elect to leave the ship while in port for an overnight trip. Just think, no moving from one hotel to another as you tour the world. So don't be too concerned about the nature of your luggage. All you need is something sturdy enough to hold your clothing and equipment safely until you reach your stateroom and again at the end of your cruise until you reach your home. For those who enjoy spending time at the beach in ports of call we suggest that one piece of light luggage be available for carrying towels, bathing suit, camera, etc. on such an outing. A flight bag or something similar works well. If this isn't feasible, then a plastic shopping bag is a good alternative.

Call Before Leaving Home

Cargo is king! Schedules, particularly on general cargo ships, are constantly modified to accommodate the requirements of the cargo. Embarkation dates projected one or two months in advance are not only subject to change, they will change, perhaps several times, between the offer of space and the time you walk up the gangplank. During the final two weeks before leaving you are likely to have two or three date changes. Don't be lulled into assuming that each change will be a postponement to a later departure date. Early changes are more

likely to be postponements but changes nearer the end can just as easily be advances to a slightly earlier date. Be ready! If you are sailing on a container ship in intercontinental liner service projected embarkation dates tend to be much firmer. Container shipping is selling reliability and speed of service. Dates by which containers must be received at the port and dates for loading and delivery are projected well in advance and the shipping companies do everything in their power to adhere to their published schedules. Our best advice is to stay in close contact with the agent and be sure to call for confirmation before leaving home. An eleventh hour postponement could cost you unnecessary dollars in hotel and meal expense as you wait for your ship. There could even be a last minute change in the port of embarkation so call to make sure.

When you reach your ship don't be dismayed if she appears grimy. Port time is a time when cargo ships accumulate dirt. The first day at sea the deckhouse and decks will be hosed down, deck chairs will be made available, and everything will be cleaned up for the passage. We hope you have a wonderful time; *bon voyage!*

CARGO SHIP CRUISING